Fishe

COLLECTI

AND

THE DREAM OF GERONTIUS

John Henry Newman was born in London in 1801, the eldest of six children of a London banker. He was educated at Ealing School and Trinity College, Oxford. In 1822 he was elected a Fellow of Oriel College. He subsequently took Anglican orders, and in 1828 was appointed Vicar of the Oxford University Church of St Mary where his skill as a preacher gave him wide influence. In the 1830s, he became a key figure in the Tractarian Movement which sought to emphasise the Catholic aspects of the Church of England's inheritance. The Movement encountered increasing opposition from Anglican authorities in the late 1830s, and in 1841, their *Tract* 90, which sought to reconcile the Anglican Church's 39 Articles with Catholic teaching, was condemned by the Oxford Heads of Houses. Newman's doubts about the validity of a "middle way" between the Catholic Church and Protestantism, kept recurring, and in 1842 he retired to the parish of Littlemore to reflect. He resigned his living of St Mary in 1843, and his Oriel fellowship in 1845, just before being received into the Catholic Church by the Passionist, the Blessed Dominic Barbieri. After training in Rome he was ordained a Catholic priest in 1847, and in 1848 founded the Birmingham Oratory, which was his home for the rest of his life. He became first rector of the Catholic University of Ireland in 1851, and founded the Oratory School in 1859. He was elected a Fellow of Trinity College, Oxford in 1877, and was created a Cardinal of the Catholic Church in 1879. He died in 1890, and is buried at Rednal, near Birmingham. A Declaration on the heroic nature of his virtues was made by the Catholic Church in 1991, a stage on the route to beatification.

His major religious and philosophical writings include: *The Arians of the Fourth Century* (1832), *Parochial and Plain Sermons* (1837), *An Essay on the Development of Christian Doctrine* (1844), *Apologia Pro Vita Sua* (1864)— a defence of his religious opinions against Charles Kingsley's attack—, an *Essay in Aid of a Grammar of Assent* (1870), and *The Idea of a University* (1874). He wrote two novels: *Loss and Gain* (1847) and *Callista* (1856). His *Verses on Various Occasions*, first published in 1868, includes his dramatic poem, *The Dream of Gerontius*, first published in 1865.

JOHN HENRY NEWMAN

COLLECTED POEMS

AND

THE DREAM OF GERONTIUS

Illustrated by Mary Tyler

cui pauca relicti
Jugera ruris erant; nec fertilis illa juvencis
Nec pecori opportuna seges, nec commoda Baccho.
Hic rarum tamen in dumis olus, albaque circum
Lilia, verbenasque premens, vescumque papaver,
Regum aequabat opes animis.

Fisher Press

Published by Fisher Press, Post Office Box 41.
Sevenoaks, Kent TN15 6YN, England

Verses on Various Occasions was first published in 1868
First issued as a Fisher Press paperback 1992

British Library Cataloguing in Publication Data
A catalogue record for this book is available from
The British Library

ISBN 1 874037 02 7

Typeset by Grand Designs, 88 Barons Court Rd, London
Printed and bound in Great Britain by
CPI Antony Rowe, Chippenham and Eastbourne
Cover: Brown, Knight & Truscott, Tunbridge Wells, Kent

ORIGINAL DEDICATION IN THE 1868 EDITION

TO EDWARD BADELEY, ESQ.

My Dear Badeley,

I have not been without apprehension lest, in dedicating to you a number of poetical compositions, I should hardly be making a suitable offering to a member of a grave profession, which is especially employed in rubbing off the gloss with which imagination and sentiment invest matters of every-day life, and in reducing statements of fact to their legitimate dimensions. And, besides this, misgivings have not unnaturally come over me on the previous question; viz., whether, after all, the contents of the volume are of sufficient importance to make it an acceptable offering to any friend whatever.

And I must frankly confess, as to the latter difficulty, that certainly it never would have occurred to me thus formally to bring together into one effusions which I have ever considered ephemeral, had I not lately found from publications of the day, what I never suspected before, that there are critics, and they strangers to me, who think well both of some of my compositions and of my power of composing. It is this commendation, bestowed on me to my surprise as well as to my gratification, which has encouraged me just now to republish what I have from time to time written; and if, in doing so, I shall be found, as is not unlikely, to have formed a volume of unequal merit, my excuse must be, that I despair of discovering any standard by which to discriminate aright between one poetical attempt and another. Accordingly, I am thrown, from the nature of the case, whether I will or no, upon my own judgment, which, biassed by the associations of memory and by personal feelings, and measuring, perhaps, by the pleasure of verse-making, the worth of the verse, is disposed either to preserve them all, or to put them all aside.

Here another contrast presents itself between the poetical art and the science of law. Your profession has its definitive authorities, its prescriptions, its precedents, and its principles, by which to determine the claim of its authors on public attention; but what philosopher will undertake to rule matters of taste, or to bring under one idea or method works so different from each other as those of Homer, Æschylus, and Pindar; of Terence, Ovid, Juvenal, and Martial? What court is sitting, and what code is received, for the satisfactory determination of the poetical pretensions of writers of the day? Whence can we hope to gain a verdict upon them, except from the unscientific tribunals of Public Opinion and of Time? In Poetry, as in Metaphysics, a book is of necessity a venture.

And now, coming to the suitableness of my offering, I know well, my dear Badeley, how little you will be disposed to criticize what comes to you from me, whatever be its intrinsic value. Less still in this case, considering that a chief portion of the volume grew out of that Religious Movement which you yourself, as well as I, so faithfully followed from first to last. And least of all, when I tell you that I wish it to be the poor expression, long-delayed, of my gratitude, never intermitted, for the great services which you rendered to me years ago, by your legal skill and affectionate zeal, in a serious matter in which I found myself in collision with the law of the land. Those services I have ever desired in some public, however inadequate, way to record; and now, as time hurries on and opportunities are few, I am forced to ask you to acknowledge my debt to you as I can, since I cannot as I would.

We are now, both of us, in the decline of life: may that warm attachment which has lasted between us inviolate for so many years, be continued, by the mercy of God, to the end of our earthly course, and beyond it!

I am, my dear Badeley,
Affectionately yours,

J.H.N.

The Oratory. *December 21, 1867.*

ACKNOWLEDGEMENTS

We are grateful to the Trustees of the Tate Gallery for permission to reproduce the watercolour, Amalfi, by J M W Turner on the cover. This sketch of a small boat off the Italian coast is from a sketchbook recording Turner's visit to Italy in 1828. It was the basis for one of the engravings after Turner which illustrated Samuel Roger's *Italy*, a topographical and historical evocation by a London lawyer. With its striking illustrations, the work did much to boost interest in the Italian tour among the English in the late 1820s and 30s. Newman's first visit to Italy was in 1833. It was at sea, while returning on an orange boat from Sicily, where he had almost died from a bout of typhoid fever, that he wrote his poem,"The Pillar and the Cloud", better known by its opening words,'Lead, Kindly Light'. We are also grateful to the Trustees of the National Portrait Gallery for permission to reproduce George Richmond's chalk drawing of Newman in the vignette.

Contents

EDITORIAL NOTE

This edition of Newman's *Collected Poems* in English is largely based on the 1888 edition of Newman's *Verses on Various Occasions*. It includes Newman's revisions to some of the poems in the first edition of 1868, and the text of five additional poems not included in the earlier edition. The five additional poems have been placed together in this edition, just before "*The Dream of Gerontius*". Apart from this, only one or two minor changes have been made to the order of the poems as arranged in the 1888 edition; a few small textual errors have also been corrected. Newman's Latin poems are not included in this edition.

SOLITUDE

THERE is in stillness oft a magic power
To calm the breast, when struggling passions lower;
Touch'd by its influence, in the soul arise
Diviner feelings, kindred with the skies.
By this the Arab's kindling thoughts expand,
When circling skies inclose the desert sand;
For this the hermit seeks the thickest grove,
To catch th' inspiring glow of heavenly love.
It is not solely in the freedom given
To purify and fix the heart on heaven;
There is a Spirit singing aye in air,
That lifts us high above all mortal care.
No mortal measure swells that mystic sound.
No mortal minstrel breathes such tones around,—
The Angels' hymn,—the sovereign harmony
That guides the rolling orbs along the sky,—
And hence perchance the tales of saints who view'd
And heard Angelic choirs in solitude.
By most unheard,—because the earthly din
Of toil or mirth has charms their ears to win.
Alas for man! he knows not of the bliss,
The heaven that brightens such a life as this.

Oxford. *Michælmas Term, 1818.*

PARAPHRASE

OF ISAIAH, CHAP. LXIV

O THAT Thou wouldest rend the breadth of sky,
That veils Thy presence from the sons of men!
O that, as erst Thou camest from on high
Sudden in strength, Thou so would'st come again!
Track'd out by judgments was Thy fiery path,
Ocean and mountain withering in Thy wrath!

Then would Thy name—the Just, the Merciful—
Strange dubious attributes to human mind,
Appal Thy foes; and, kings, who spurn Thy rule,
Then, then would quake to hopeless doom consign'd.
See, the stout bows, and totters the secure,
While pleasure's bondsman hides his head impure!

Come down! for then shall from its seven bright springs
To him who thirsts the draught of life be given;
Eye hath not seen, ear hath not heard the things
Which He hath purposed for the heirs of heaven,—
A God of love, guiding with gracious ray
Each meek rejoicing pilgrim on his way.

Yea, though we err, and Thine averted face
Rebukes the folly in Thine Isræl done,
Will not that hour of chastisement give place
To beams, the pledge of an eternal sun?
Yes! for His counsels to the end endure;
We shall be saved, our rest abideth sure.

Lord, Lord! our sins...our sins...unclean are we,
Gross and corrupt; our seeming-virtuous deeds
Are but abominate; all, dead to Thee,
Shrivel, like leaves when summer's green recedes;
While, like the autumn blast, our lusts arise,
And sweep their prey where the fell serpent lies.

None, there is none to plead with God in prayer,
Bracing his laggart spirit to the work
Of intercession; conscience-sprung despair,
Sin-loving still, doth in each bosom lurk.
Guilt calls Thee to avenge;—Thy risen ire
Sears like a brand, we gaze and we expire.

But now, O Lord, our Father! we are Thine,
    Design and fashion; senseless while we lay,
Thou, as the potter, with a Hand Divine,
    Didst mould Thy vessels of the sluggish clay.
Mark not our guilt, Thy word of wrath recall,
Lo, we are Thine by price, Thy people all!

Alas for Zion! 'tis a waste;—the fair,
    The holy place in flames;—where once our sires
Kindled the sacrifice of praise and prayer,
    Far other brightness gleams from Gentile fires.
Low lies our pride;—and wilt Thou self-deny
Thy rescuing arm, unvex'd amid Thine Israel's cry?

Brighton *September, 1821.*

TO F.W.N.

A BIRTHDAY OFFERING

DEAR Frank, this morn has usher'd in
    The manhood of thy days;
A boy no more, thou must begin
    To choose thy future ways;
To brace thy arm, and nerve thy heart,
For maintenance of a noble part.

And thou a voucher fair hast given,
    Of what thou wilt achieve,
Ere age has dimm'd thy sun-lit heaven
    In weary life's chill eve;
Should Sovereign Wisdom in its grace
Vouchsafe to thee so long a race.

My brother, we are link'd with chain
    That time shall ne'er destroy;
Together we have been in pain,
    Together now in joy;
For duly I to share may claim
The present brightness of thy name.

My brother, 'tis no recent tie
  Which binds our fates in one,
E'en from our tender infancy
  The twisted thread was spun;—
Her deed, who stored in her fond mind
Our forms, by sacred love enshrined.

In her affection all had share,
  All six, she loved them all;
Yet on her early-chosen Pair
  Did her full favour fall;
And we became her dearest theme,
Her waking thought, her nightly dream.

Ah! brother, shall we e'er forget
  Her love, her care, her zeal?
We cannot pay the countless debt,
  But we must ever feel;
For through her earnestness were shed
Prayer-purchased blessings on our head.

Though in the end of days she stood,
  And pain and weakness came,
Her force of thought was unsubdued,
  Her fire of love the same;
And e'en when memory fail'd its part,
We still kept lodgment in her heart.

And when her Maker from the thrall
  Of flesh her spirit freed,
Nor suffering companied the call,
  —In mercy 'twas decreed,—
One moment here, the next she trod
The viewless mansion of her God.

Now then at length she is at rest,
  And, after many a woe,
Rejoices in that Saviour blest,
  Who was her hope below;
Kept till the day when He shall own
His saints before His Father's throne.

So it is left for us to prove
   Her prayers were not in vain;
And that God's grace-according love
   Has come as gentle rain,
Which, falling in the vernal hour,
Tints the young leaf, perfumes the flower.

Dear Frank, we both are summon'd now
   As champions of the Lord;—
Enroll'd am I, and shortly thou
   Must buckle on thy sword;
A high employ, nor lightly given,
To serve as messengers of heaven!

Deep in my heart that gift I hide;
   I change it not away
For patriot-warrior's hour of pride,
   Or statesman's tranquil sway;
For poet's fire, or pleader's skill
To pierce the soul and tame the will.

O! may we follow undismay'd
   Where'er our God shall call!
And may his Spirit's present aid
   Uphold us lest we fall!
Till in the end of days we stand,
As victors in a deathless land.

Chiswick. *June 27, 1826.*

NATURE AND ART

FOR AN ALBUM

"MAN goeth forth[1]" with reckless trust
   Upon his wealth of mind,
As if in self a thing of dust
   Creative skill might find;
He schemes and toils; stone, wood, and ore
Subject or weapon of his power.

By arch and spire, by tower-girt heights,
   He would his boast fulfil;
By marble births, and mimic lights,—
   Yet lacks one secret still;
Where is the master-hand shall give
To breathe, to move, to speak, to live?

O take away this shade of might,
  The puny toil of man,
And let rich Nature in my sight
  Unroll her gorgeous plan;
I cannot bear those sullen walls,
Those eyeless towers, those tongueless halls.

Art's labour'd toys of highest name
  Are nerveless, cold, and dumb;
And man is fitted but to frame
  A coffin or a tomb;
Well suits when sense has pass'd away,
Such lifeless works the lifeless clay.

Here let me sit where wooded hills
  Skirt yon far-reaching plain;
While cattle bank its winding rills,
  And suns embrown its grain;
Such prospect is to me right dear,
For freedom, health, and joy are here.

There is a spirit ranging through
  The earth, the stream, the air;
Ten thousand shapes, garbs ever new,
  That restless One doth wear;
In colour, scent, and taste, and sound
The energy of Life is found.

The leaves are rustling in the breeze,
  The bird renews her song;
From field to brook, o'er heath, o'er trees,
  The sunbeam glides along;
The insect, happy in its hour,
Floats softly by, or sips the flower.

Now dewy rain descends, and now
  Brisk showers the welkin shroud;
I care not, though with angry brow
  Frowns the red thunder-cloud;
Let hail-storm pelt, and lightning harm,
'Tis Nature's work, and has its charm.

Ah! lovely Nature! others dwell
Full favour'd in thy court;
I of thy smiles but hear them tell,
And feed on their report,
Catching what glimpse an Ulcombe yields
To strangers loitering in her fields.

I go where form has ne'er unbent
The sameness of its sway;
Where iron rule, stern precedent,
Mistreat the graceful day;
To pine as prisoner in his cell,
And yet be thought to love it well.

Yet so His high dispose has set,
Who binds on each his part;
Though absent, I may cherish yet
An Ulcombe of the heart;
Calm verdant hope divinely given,
And suns of peace, and scenes of heaven;—

A soul prepared His will to meet,
Full fix'd His work to do;
Not labour'd into sudden heat,
But inly born anew.—
So living Nature, not dull Art,
Shall plan my ways and rule my heart.

Ulcombe. *September*, 1826.

[1] Psalm civ.(ciii.) 23.

INTRODUCTION

TO AN ALBUM

I AM a harp of many chords, and each
Strung by a separate hand;—most musical
My notes, discoursing with the mental sense,
Not the outward ear. Try them, they will reply
With wisdom, fancy, graceful gaiety,
Or ready wit, or happy sentiment.

Come, add a string to my assort of sounds;
Widen the compass of my harmony;
And join thyself in fellowship of name
With those, whose courteous labour and fair gifts
Have given me voice, and made me what I am.

Brighton. *April, 1827.*

SNAPDRAGON

A RIDDLE FOR A FLOWER BOOK

I AM rooted in the wall
Of buttress'd tower or ancient hall;
Prison'd in an art-wrought bed,
Cased in mortar, cramp'd with lead;
Of a living stock alone
Brother of the lifeless stone.

Else unprized, I have my worth
On the spot that gives me birth;
Nature's vast and varied field
Braver flowers than me will yield,
Bold in form and rich in hue,
Children of a purer dew;
Smiling lips and winning eyes
Meet for earthly paradise.

Choice are such,—and yet thou knowest
Highest he whose lot is lowest.
They, proud hearts, a home reject
Framed by human architect;
Humble-I can bear to dwell
Near the pale recluse's cell,
And I spread my crimson bloom,
Mingled with the cloister's gloom.

Life's gay gifts and honours rare,
Flowers of favour! win and wear!
Rose of beauty, be the queen
In pleasure's ring and festive scene.
Ivy, climb and cluster, where
Lordly oaks vouchsafe a stair.
Vaunt, fair Lily, stately dame,
Pride of birth and pomp of name.
Miser Crocus, starved with cold,
Hide in earth thy timid gold.
Travell'd Dahlia, freely boast
Knowledge brought from foreign coast.
Pleasure, wealth, birth, knowledge, power,
These have each an emblem flower;
So for me alone remains
Lowly thought and cheerful pains.

Be it mine to set restraint
On roving wish and selfish plaint;
And for man's drear haunts to leave
Dewy morn and balmy eve.
Be it mine the barren stone
To deck with green life not its own,

So to soften and to grace
Of human works the rugged face.
Mine, the Unseen to display
In the crowded public way,
Where life's busy arts combine
To shut out the Hand Divine.

Ah! no more a scentless flower,
By approving Heaven's high power,
Suddenly my leaves exhale
Fragrance of the Syrian gale.
Ah! 'tis timely comfort given
By the answering breath of Heaven!
May it be! then well might I
In College cloister live and die.

Ulcombe. *October 2, 1827.*

THE TRANCE OF TIME

Felix, qui potuit rerum cognoscere causas,
Atque metus omnes, et inexorabile fatum
Subjecit pedibus, strepitumque Acherontis avari!

IN childhood, when with eager eyes
The season-measure year I view'd
All, garb'd in fairy guise,
Pledged constancy of good.

Spring sang of heaven; the summer flowers
Bade me gaze on, and did not fade;
Even suns o'er autumn's bowers
Heard my strong wish, and stay'd.

They came and went, the short-lived four;
Yet, as their varying dance they wove,
To my young heart each bore
Its own sure claim of love.

Far different now;—the whirling year
Vainly my dizzy eyes pursue;
And its fair tints appear
All blent in one dusk hue.

Why dwell on rich autumnal lights,
  Spring-time, or winter's social ring?
    Long days are fire-side nights,
      Brown autumn is fresh spring.

Then what this world to thee, my heart?
  Its gifts nor feed thee nor can bless.
    Thou hast no owner's part
      In all its fleetingness.

The flame, the storm, the quaking ground,
  Earth's joy, earth's terror, nought is thine;
    Thou must but hear the sound
      Of the still voice divine.

O priceless art! O princely state!
  E'en while by sense of change opprest,
    Within to antedate
      Heaven's Age of fearless rest.

Highwood. *October, 1827.*

CONSOLATIONS IN BEREAVEMENT

DEATH was full urgent with thee, Sister dear,
  And startling in his speed;—
Brief pain, then langour till thy end came near—
  Such was the path decreed,
    The hurried road
To lead thy soul from earth to thine own God's abode.

Death wrought with thee, sweet main, impatiently:—
  Yet merciful the haste
That baffles sickness;—dearest, thou didst die,
  Thou wast not made to taste
    Death's bitterness,
Decline's slow-wasting charm, or fever's fierce distress.

Death came unheralded:—but it was well;
  For so thy Saviour bore
Kind witness, thou wast meet at once to dwell
  On His eternal shore;
    All warning spared,
For none He gives where hearts are for prompt change prepared.

Death wrought in mystery; both complaint and cure
  To human skill unknown:—
God put aside all means, to make us sure
  It was His deed alone;
    Lest we should lay
Reproach on our poor selves, that thou wast caught away.

Death urged as scant of time:—lest, Sister dear,
  We many a lingering day
Had sicken'd with alternate hope and fear,
  The ague of delay;
    Watching each spark
Of promise quench'd in turn, till all our sky was dark.

Death came and went:—that so thy image might
  Our yearning hearts possess,
Associate with all pleasant thoughts and bright,
  With youth and loveliness;
    Sorrow can claim,
Mary, nor lot nor part in thy soft soothing name.

Joy of sad hearts, and light of downcast eyes!
  Dearest, thou art enshrined
In all thy fragrance in our memories;
  For we must ever find
    Bare thought of thee
Freshen this weary life, while weary life shall be.

Oxford. *April, 1828.*

A PICTURE

The maiden is not dead, but sleepeth.

SHE is not gone;—still in our sight
That dearest maid shall live,
In form as true, in tints as bright,
  As youth and health could give.

Still, still is ours the modest eye;
  The smile unwrought by art;
The glance that shot so piercingly
  Affection's keenest dart;

The thrilling voice, I ne'er could hear
    But felt a joy and pain;—
A pride that she was ours, a fear
    Ours she might not remain;

Whether the page divine called forth
    Its clear, sweet, tranquil tone,
Or cheerful hymn, or seemly mirth
    In sprightlier measure shown;

The meek inquiry of that face,
    Musing on wonders found,
As 'mid dim paths she sought to trace
    The truth on sacred ground;

The thankful sigh that would arise,
    When aught her doubts removed,
Full sure the explaining voice to prize,
    Admiring while she loved;

The pensive brow, the world might see
    When she in crowds was found;
The burst of heart, the o'erflowing glee
    When only friends were round;

Hope's warmth of promise, prompt to fill
    The thoughts with good in store,
Match'd with content's deep stream, which still
    Flow'd on, when hope was o'er;

That peace, which, with its own bright day,
    Made cheapest sights shine fair;
That purest grace, which track'd its way
    Safe from aught earthly there.

Such was she in the sudden hour
    That brought her Maker's call,—
Proving her heart's self-mastering power
    Blithely to part with all,—

All her eye loved, all her hand press'd
    With keen affection's flow,
The voice of home, all pleasures best,
    All dearest thoughts below.

From friend-lit hearth, from social board,
  All duteously she rose;
For faith upon the Master's word
  Can find a sure repose.

And in her wonder up she sped,
  And tried relief in vain;
Then laid her down upon her bed
  Of languor and of pain,—

And waited till the solemn spell,
  (A ling'ring night and day,)
Should fill its numbers, and compel
  Her soul to come away.

Such was she then; and such she is,
  Shrined in each mourner's breast;
Such shall she be, and more than this,
  In promised glory blest;

When in due lines her Saviour dear
  His scatter'd saints shall range,
And knit in love souls parted here,
  Where cloud is none, nor change.

Oxford. *August, 1828.*

MY LADY NATURE AND HER DAUGHTERS

LADIES, well I deem, delight
  In comely tire to move;
Soft, and delicate, and bright,
  Are the robes they love.
Silks, where hues alternate play,
Shawls, and scarfs, and mantles gay,
Gold, and gems, and crispèd hair,
Fling their light o'er lady fair.
'Tis not waste, nor sinful pride,
—Name them not, nor fault beside,—
But her very cheerfulness
Prompts and weaves the curious dress;

While her holy[1] thoughts still roam
Mid birth-friends and scenes of home.
Pleased to praise whose praise is dear,
Glitters she? she glitters there;—
And she has a pattern found her
In Nature's glowing world around her.

Nature loves, as lady bright,
    In gayest guise to shine,
All forms of grace, all tints of light,
    Fringe her robe divine.
Sun-lit heaven, and rainbow cloud,
Changeful main, and mountain proud,
Branching tree, and meadow green,
All are deck'd in broider'd sheen.
Not a bird on bough-propp'd tower,
Insect slim, nor tiny flower,
Stone, nor spar, nor shell of sea,
But is fair in its degree.
'Tis not pride, this vaunt of beauty;
Well she 'quits her trust of duty;
And, amid her gorgeous state,
Bright, and bland, and delicate,
Ever beaming from her face
Praise of a Father's love we trace.

Ladies, shrinking from the view
    Of the prying day,
In tranquil diligence pursue
    Their heaven-appointed way.
Noiseless duties, silent cares,
Mercies lighting unawares,
Modest influence working good,
Gifts, by the keen heart understood,
Such as viewless spirits might give,
These they love, in these they live.—
Mighty Nature speeds her through
Her daily toils in silence too;
Calmly rolls her giant spheres,
Sheds by stealth her dew's kind tears;

Cheating sage's vex'd pursuit,
Churns the sap, matures the fruit,
And, her deft hand still concealing,
Kindles motion, life and feeling.

Ladies love to laugh and sing,
  To rouse the chord's full sound,
Or to join the festive ring
  Where dancers gather round.
Not a sight so fair on earth,
As a lady's graceful mirth;
Not a sound so chasing pain,
As a lady's thrilling strain.—
Nor is Nature left behind
In her lighter moods of mind;
Calm her duties to fulfil,
In her glee a prattler still.
Bird and beast of every sort
Hath its antic and its sport;
Chattering brook, and dancing gnat,
Subtle cry of evening bat,
Moss uncouth, and twigs grotesque,
These are Nature's picturesque.

Where the birth of Poesy?
  Its fancy and its fire?
Nature's earth, and sea, and sky,
  Fervid thoughts inspire.
Where do wealth and power find rest,
When hopes have failèd, or toil oppress'd?
Parks, and lawns, and deer, and trees,
Nature's work, restore them ease.—
Rare the rich, the gifted rare,—
Where shall work-day souls repair,
Unennobled, unrefined,
From the rude world and unkind?
Who shall friend their lowly lot?
High-born Nature answers not.

Leave her in her starry dome,
Seek we lady-lighted home.
Nature 'mid the spheres holds sway,
Ladies rule where hearts obey.

Oxford. *February 4, 1829.*

[1] Vid. 1 Pet. iii.5; and cf. Gen. xxiv, 22, 28-30.

OPUSCULUM.

FOR A VERY SMALL ALBUM.

FAIR Cousin, thy page
is small to encage
the thoughts which engage
the mind of a sage
such as I am;

'Twere in teaspoon to take
the whole Genevese lake,
or a lap-dog to make
the white Elephant sac-
-red in Siam.

Yet inadequate though
to the terms strange and so-
-lemn that figure in po-
-lysyllabical row
in a treatise;

Still, true words and plain,
of the heart, not the brain,
in affectionate strain,
this book to contain
very meet is.

So I promise to be
a good Cousin to thee,
and to keep safe the se-
cret I heard, although e-
-v'ry one know it;

With a lyrical air
my kind thoughts I would dare,
and offer whate'er
beseems the news, were
I a poet.

Brighton. *April, 1829.*

A VOICE FROM AFAR

WEEP not for me;—
Be blithe as wont, nor tinge with gloom
The stream of love that circles home,
Light hearts and free!
Joy in the gifts Heaven's bounty lends;
Nor miss my face, dear friends!

I still am near;—
Watching the smiles I prized on earth,
Your converse mild, your blameless mirth;
Now too I hear
Of whisper'd sounds the tale complete,
Low prayers, and musings sweet.

A sea before
The Throne is spread;—its pure still glass
Pictures all earth-scenes as they pass.
We, on its shore,
Share, in the bosom of our rest,
God's knowledge, and are blest.

Horsepath. *September 29, 1829.*

THE HIDDEN ONES

HID are the saints of God;—
Uncertified by high angelic sign;
Nor raiment soft, nor empire's golden rod
Marks them divine.
Theirs but the unbought air, earth's parent sod,
And the sun's smile benign;—
Christ rears His throne within the secret heart,
From the haughty world apart.

They gleam amid the night,
Chill sluggish mists stifling the heavenly ray;
Fame chants the while,—old history trims his light,
Aping the day;
In vain! staid look, loud voice, and reason's might
Forcing its learned way,
Blind characters! these aid us not to trace
Christ and His princely race.

Yet not all-hid from those
Who watch to see;—'neath their dull guise of earth,
Bright bursting gleams unwittingly disclose
Their heaven-wrought birth.
Meekness, love, patience, faith's serene repose;
And the soul's tutor'd mirth,
Bidding the slow heart dance, to prove her power
O'er self in its proud hour.

These are the chosen few,
The remnant fruit of largely-scatter'd grace,
God sows in waste, to reap whom He foreknew
Of man's cold race;
Counting on wills perverse, in His clear view
Of boundless time and space,
He waits, by scant return for treasures given,
To fill the thrones of heaven.

Lord! who can trace but Thou
The strife obscure, 'twixt sin's soul-thralling spell
And Thy sharp Spirit, now quench'd, reviving now?
Or who can tell,
Why pardon's seal stands sure on David's brow,
Why Saul and Demas fell?
Oh! lest our frail hearts in the annealing break,
Help, for Thy mercy's sake!

Horsepath. *September, 1829.*

A THANKSGIVING

Thou in faithfulness hast afflicted me.

LORD, in this dust Thy sovereign voice
First quicken'd love divine;
I am all Thine,—Thy care and choice,
My very praise is Thine.

I praise Thee, while Thy providence
In childhood frail I trace,
For blessings given, ere dawning sense
Could seek or scan Thy grace;

Blessings in boyhood's marvelling hour,
Bright dreams, and fancyings strange;
Blessings, when reason's awful power
Gave thought a bolder range;

Blessings of friends, which to my door
Unask'd, unhoped, have come;
And, choicer still, a countless store
Of eager smiles at home.

Yet, Lord, in memory's fondest place
I shrine those seasons sad,
When, looking up, I saw Thy face
In kind austereness clad.

I would not miss one sigh or tear,
Heart-pang, or throbbing brow;
Sweet was the chastisement severe,
And sweet its memory now.

Yes! let the fragrant scars abide,
Love-tokens in Thy stead,
Faint shadows of the spear-pierced side
And thorn-encompass'd head.

And such Thy tender force be still,
When self would swerve or stray,
Shaping to truth the froward will
Along Thy narrow way.

Deny me wealth; far, far remove
The lure of power or name;
Hope thrives in straits, in weakness love,
And faith in this world's shame.

Oxford. *October, 1829.*

MONK.

FOR ANOTHER SMALL ALBUM

(With lines on hinges to fit it.)

WHY, dear Cousin,
why
Ask for verses,
when a poet's
fount of song is
dry?
Or, if aught be
there,
Harsh and chill, it
ill may touch the
hand of lady
fair.
Who can perfumed waters
bring
From a convent
spring?
"Monks in the olden
time,
"They were rhymesters?"—
they were rhymesters,
but in Latin
rhyme.
Monks in the days of
old
Lived in secret,
in the Church's
kindly-sheltering
fold.

No bland meditators
they
Of a courtly
lay.

"They had visions
bright?"—
they had visions,
yet not sent in
slumbers soft and
light.
No! a lesson
stern,
First by vigils,
fast, and penance,
theirs it was to
learn.
This their soul-ennobling
gain,
Joys wrought out by
pain.

"When from home they
stirr'd,
"Sweet their voices?"—
still, a blessing
closed their merriest
word;
And their gayest
smile
Told of musings
solitary,
and the hallow'd
aisle.

"Songsters?"—hark! they answer!
round
Plaintive chantings
sound!

Grey his cowlèd
vest,
Whose strong heart has
pledged his service
to the cloister
blest.
Duly garb'd is
he,
As the frost-work
gems the branches
of yon stately
tree
'Tis a danger-thwarting
spell,
And it fits me
well!

Oxford. *December, 1829.*

EPIPHANY-EVE

A BIRTHDAY OFFERING

BIRTHDAY gifts, with the early year,
Lo! we bring thee, Mary dear!
Prayer and praise upon thy death
Twined together in a wreath,
Grief and gladness, such as may
Suit a solemn holiday.
Christmas snow, for maiden's bloom
Blanched in winter's sudden tomb;
Christmas berries, His red token
Who that grave's stern seal hath broken;
These for thee the faithful heart,
Due mementos, sets apart.

'Twas a fast, that Eve of sorrow,
Herald veil'd of glorious morrow.
Speechless we sat; and watch'd, to know
How it would be; but time moved slow,
Along that day of sacred woe.

Then came the Feast, and we were told
Bravely of our best to bring,
Myrrh, and frankincense, and gold,
As our tribute to our King.

Dearest, gentlest, purest, best!
Deep is thy mysterious rest,
Now the solemn hours are over
And the Angels round thee hover,
With the fanning of their wings
Keeping time to one who sings
Of high themes consolatory,
Of the All-loving and His glory,
Of the age that has no ending,
Of the day of thy ascending
From those shades of paradise
To the bright supernal skies.

Thinkest of us, dearest, ever?
Ah! so be it nought can sever
Spirit and life, the past and present,
Still we yield thee musings pleasant.
—God above, and we below;—
So thought ranges, to and fro.
He, in sooth, by tutorings mild,
From the rude clay shaped His child,
Fiery trial, anguish chill,
Served not here His secret will;
But His voice was low and tender,
And so true was thy surrender,
That the work in haste was done,
Grace and nature blent in one.—
Harmless thus, and not unmeet,
To kiss the dear prints of thy feet,
Tracing thus the narrow road
All must tread, and Christ has trod.

Loveliest, meekest, blithest, kindest!
Lead! we seek the home thou findest!
Though thy name to us most dear,
Go! we would not have thee here.

Lead, a guiding beacon bright
To travellers on the Eve of Light.
Welcome aye thy Star before us,
Bring it grief or gladness o'er us;—
Keen regret and tearful yearning,
Whiles unfelt, and whiles returning;—
Or more gracious thoughts abiding,
Fever-quelling, sorrow-chiding;—
Or, when day-light blessings fail,
Transport fresh as spice-fraught gale,
Sparks from thee, which oft have lighted
Weary heart and hope benighted.

I this monument would raise,
Distant from the public gaze.
Few will see it;—few e'er knew thee;
But their beating hearts pursue thee,—
And their eyes fond thoughts betoken,
Though thy name be seldom spoken.
Pass on, stranger, and despise it!
These will read, and these will prize it.

Oxford. *January 5, 1830.*

THE WINTER FLOWER

A BIRTHDAY OFFERING

(For Music.)

BLOOM, beloved Flower!—
  Unknown;—'tis no matter.
Courts glitter brief hour,
  Crowds can but flatter.

Plants in the garden
  See best the Sun's glory;
They miss the green sward in
  A conservatory.

—PRIZED WHERE'ER KNOWN.—
  Sure this is a blessing,
Outrings the loud tone
  Of the dull world's caressing.

Oxford. *December 30, 1830.*

KIND REMEMBRANCES

TIS long, dear Annie, since we met,
Yet deem not that my heart,
For all that absence, can forget
A kinsman's pious part.

How oft on thee, a sufferer mild,
My kindly thoughts I turn,
He knows, upon whose altar piled
The prayers of suppliants burn.

I love thy name, admiring all
Thy sacred heaven-sent pain;
I love it, for it seems to call
The Lost to earth again.

Can I forget, *she* to thy need
Her ministry supplied,
Who now, from mortal duty freed,
Serves at the Virgin's side?

What would'st thou more? Upon thy head
A two-fold grace is pour'd;—
Both in thyself, and for the dead,
A witness of thy Lord!

Oxford. *March*, 1831.

SEEDS IN THE AIR

FOR AN ALBUM

Igneus est ollis vigor, et cœlestis origo
Seminibus.

COULD I hit on a theme
To fashion my verse on,
Not long would I seem
A lack-courtesy person.
But I have not the skill,
Nor talisman strong,
To summon at will
The Spirit of song.—
Bright thoughts are roaming

Unseen in the air;
Like comets, their coming
Is sudden and rare.
They strike, and they enter,
And light up the brain,
Which thrills to its centre
With rapturous pain.
Where the chance-seed
Is piously nursed,
Brighter succeed
In the path of the first.—
One sighs to the Muse,
Or the sweet nightingale,
One sips the night-dews
Which moon-beams exhale.
All this is a fiction;
I never could find
A suitable friction
To frenzy my mind.
What use are empirics?
No gas on their shelf
Can made one spout lyrics
In spite of oneself!

Dartington. *July 18, 1831.*

THE PILGRIM

FOR AN ALBUM

THERE stray'd awhile, amid the woods of Dart,
One who could love them, but who durst not love.
A vow had bound him, ne'er to give his heart
To streamlet bright, or soft secluded grove.
'Twas a hard humbling task, onwards to move
His easy-captured eyes from each fair spot,
With unattach'd and lonely step to rove
O'er happy meads, which soon its print forgot:—
Yet kept he safe his pledge, prizing his pilgrim-lot.

Dartington. *July 21, 1831.*

HOME

WHERE'ER I roam in this fair English land,
The vision of a Temple meets my eyes:
   Modest without, within, all-glorious rise
Its love-encluster'd columns, and expand
Their slender arms. Like olive-plants they stand,
   Each answ'ring each, in home's soft sympathies,
   Sisters and brothers. At the altar sighs
Parental fondness, and with anxious hand
Tenders its offering of young vows and prayers.
The same, and not the same, go where I will,
The vision beams! ten thousand shrines, all one.
Dear fertile soil! what foreign culture bears
Such fruit? And I through distant climes may run
My weary round, yet miss thy likeness still.

Oxford. *November 16, 1832.*

THE BRAND OF CAIN

I BEAR upon my brow the sign
Of sorrow and of pain;
Alas! no hopeful cross is mine,
It is the brand of Cain.

The course of passion, and the fret
Of godless hope and fear,—
Toil, care, and guilt,—their hues have set,
And fix'd their sternness there.

Saviour! wash out the imprinted shame;
That I no more may pine,
Sin's martyr, though not meet to claim
Thy cross, a saint of Thine.

Oxford. *November 18, 1832.*

ZEAL AND LOVE

AND would'st thou reach, rash scholar mine,
Love's high unruffled state?
Awake! thy easy dreams resign,
First learn thee how to hate:—

Hatred of sin, and Zeal, and Fear,
Lead up the Holy Hill;
Track them, till Charity appear
A self-denial still.

Dim is the philosophic flame,
By thoughts severe unfed:
Book-lore ne'er served, when trial came,
Nor gifts, when faith was dead.

Oxford. *November 20, 1832.*

PERSECUTION

And the woman fled into the wilderness.

SAY, who is he in deserts seen,
Or at the twilight hour;
Of garb austere, and dauntless mien,
Measured in speech, in purpose keen,
Calm as in Heaven he had been,
Yet blithe when perils lower?

My Holy Mother made reply,
  "Dear child, it is my Priest.
The world has cast me forth, and I
Dwell with wild earth and gusty sky;
He bears to men my mandates high,
  And works my sage behest.

Another day, dear child, and thou
  Shalt join his sacred band.
Ah! well I deem, thou shrinkest now
From urgent rule and severing vow;
Gay hopes flit round, and light thy brow:
  Time hath a taming hand!"

Oxford. *November 22, 1832.*

ZEAL AND PURITY

Come with me, and see my zeal for the Lord.

THOU to wax fierce
  In the cause of the Lord,
To threat and to pierce
  With the heavenly sword!
Anger and Zeal,
  And the Joy of the brave,
Who bade *thee* to feel,
  Sin's slave.

The Altar's pure flame
  Consumes as it soars;
Faith meetly may blame,
  For it serves and adores.
Thou warnest and smitest!
  Yet Christ must atone
For a soul that thou slightest—
  Thine own.

Oxford. *November 23, 1832.*

THE GIFT OF PERSEVERANCE

ONCE, as I brooded o'er my guilty state,
A fever seized me, duties to devise,
To buy me interest in my Saviour's eyes;
Not that His love I would extenuate,
But scourge and penance, masterful self-hate,
Or gift of cost, served by an artifice
To quell my restless thoughts and envious sighs
And doubts, which fain heaven's peace would antedate.
Thus as I tossed, He said,—"E'en holiest deeds
Shroud not the soul from God, nor soothe its needs;
Deny thee thine own fears, and wait the end!"
Stern lesson! Let me con it day by day,
And learn to kneel before the Omniscient Ray,
Nor shrink, when Truth's avenging shafts descend!

Oxford. *November 23, 1832.*

THE SIGN OF THE CROSS

WHENE'ER across this sinful flesh of mine
I draw the Holy Sign,
All good thoughts stir within me, and renew
Their slumbering strength divine;
Till there springs up a courage high and true
To suffer and to do.

And who shall say, but hateful spirits around,
For their brief hour unbound,
Shudder to see, and wail their overthrow?
While on far heathen ground
Some lonely Saint hails the fresh odour, though
Its source he cannot know.

Oxford. *November 25, 1832.*

BONDAGE

O PROPHET, tell me not of peace,
Or Christ's all-loving deeds;
Death only can from sin release,
And death to judgment leads.

Thou from thy birth hast set thy face
  Towards thy Redeemer Lord;
To tend and deck His holy place,
  And note His secret word.

I ne'er shall reach Heaven's glorious path;
  Yet haply tears may stay
The purpose of His instant wrath,
  And slake the fiery day.

Then plead for one who cannot pray,
  Whose faith is but despair,
Who hates his heart, nor puts away
  The sin that rankles there[1].

Iffley. *November 28, 1832.*

[1] The last stanza is not as it stood originally. In this and other alterations in these compositions, care has been taken not to introduce ideas foreign to the Author's sentiments at the time of writing.

THE SCARS OF SIN

MY smile is bright, my glance is free,
  My voice is calm and clear;
Dear friend, I seem a type to thee
  Of holy love and fear.

But I am scann'd by eyes unseen,
  And these no saint surround;
They mete what is by what has been,
  And joy the lost is found.

Erst my good Angel shrank to see
  My thoughts and ways of ill;
And now he scarce dare gaze on me,
  Scar-seam'd and crippled still.

Iffley. *November 29, 1832.*

ANGELIC GUIDANCE

ARE these the tracks of some unearthly Friend,
His foot-prints, and his vesture-skirts of light,
Who, as I talk with men, conforms aright
Their sympathetic words, or deeds that blend
With my hid thought;—or stoops him to attend
My doubtful-pleading grief;—or blunts the might
Of ill I see not;—or in dreams of night
Figures the scope, in which what is will end?
Were I Christ's own, then fitly might I call
That vision real; for to the thoughful mind
That walks with Him, He half unveils His face;
But, when on earth-stain'd souls such tokens fall,
These dare not claim as theirs what there they find,
Yet, not all hopeless, eye His boundless grace.

Whitchurch. *December 3, 1832.*

SUBSTANCE AND SHADOW

THEY do but grope in learning's pedant round,
Who on the fantasies of sense bestow
An idol substance, bidding us bow low
Before those shades of being which are found,
Stirring or still, on man's brief trial-ground;
As if such shapes and moods, which come and go,
Had aught of Truth or Life in their poor show,
To sway or judge, and skill to sane or wound.
Son of immortal seed, high-destined Man!
Know thy dread gift,—a creature, yet a cause:
Each mind is its own centre, and it draws
Home to itself, and moulds in its thought's span
All outward things, the vassals of its will,
Aided by Heaven, by earth unthwarted still.

Falmouth. *December* 7, 1832.

WANDERINGS

ERE yet I left home's youthful shrine,
My heart and hope were stored
Where first I caught the rays divine,
And drank the Eternal Word.

I went afar; the world unroll'd
Her many-pictured page;
I stored the marvels which she told,
And trusted to her gage.

Her pleasures quaff'd, I sought awhile
The scenes I prized before;
But parent's praise and sister's smile
Stirr'd my cold heart no more.

So ever sear, so ever cloy
Earth's favours as they fade;
Since Adam lost for one fierce joy
His Eden's sacred shade.

Off the Lizard. *December* 8, 1832.

THE SAINT AND THE HERO

O AGED Saint! far off I heard
 The praises of thy name;—
Thy deed of power, thy prudent word,
 Thy zeal's triumphant flame.

I came and saw; and, having seen,
 Weak heart, I drew offence
From thy prompt smile, they simple mien,
 Thy lowly diligence.

The Saint's is not the Hero's praise;—
 This I have found, and learn
Nor to malign Heaven's humblest ways,
 Nor its least boon to spurn.

Bay of Biscay. *December 10, 1832.*

PRIVATE JUDGMENT

POOR wand'rers, ye are sore distress'd
To find that path which Christ has bless'd
 Track'd by His saintly throng;
Each claims to trust his own weak will,
Blind idol!—so ye languish still,
 All wranglers and all wrong.

He saw of old, and met your need,
Granting you prophets of His creed,
 The throes of fear to swage;
They fenced the rich bequest He made,
And sacred hands have safe convey'd
 Their charge from age to age.

Wand'rers! come home! obey the call!
A mother pleads, who ne'er let fall
 One grain of Holy Truth;
Warn you and win she shall and must,
For now she lifts her from the dust,
 To reign as in her youth.

Off Cape Ortegal. *December 11, 1832.*

THE WATCHMAN

(A Song.)

FAINT not, and fret not, for threaten'd woe,
  Watchman on Truth's grey height!
Few though the faithful, and fierce though the foe,
  Weakness is aye Heaven's might.

Infidel Ammon and niggard Tyre,
  Ill-fitted pair, unite;
Some work for love, and some work for hire,
  But weakness shall be Heaven's might.

Eli's feebleness, Saul's black wrath,
  May aid Ahitophel's spite;
And prayers from Gerizim, and curses from Gath—
  Our weakness shall prove Heaven's might.

Quail not, and quake not, thou Warder bold,
Be there no friend in sight;
Turn thee to question the days of old,
When weakness was aye Heaven's might.

Moses was one, but he stay'd the sin
Of the host, in the Presence bright;
And Elias scorn'd the Carmel din,
When Baal would match Heaven's might.

Time's years are many, Eternity one,
And one is the Infinite;
The chosen are few, few the deeds well done,
For scantness is still Heaven's might.

At Sea. *December 12, 1832.*

THE ISLES OF THE SIRENS

CEASE, Stranger, cease those piercing notes,
The craft of Siren choirs;
Hush the seductive voice, that floats
Upon the languid wires.

Music's ethereal fire was given,
Not to dissolve our clay,
But draw Promethean beams from heaven,
And purge the dross away.

Weak self! with thee the mischief lies,
Those throbs a tale disclose;
Nor age nor trial has made wise
The Man of many woes.

Off Lisbon. *December 13, 1832.*

ABSOLUTION

O FATHER, list a sinner's call!
Fain would I hide from man my fall—
But I must speak, or faint—
I cannot wear guilt's silent thrall:
Cleanse me, kind Saint!

"Sinner ne'er blunted yet sin's goad;
Speed thee, my son, a safer road,
And sue His pardoning smile
Who walk'd woe's depths, bearing man's load
Of guilt the while."

Yet raise a mitigating hand,
And minister some potion bland,
Some present fever-stay!
Lest one from whom His work was plann'd
Die from dismay.

"Look not to me—no grace is mine;
But I can lift the Mercy-sign.
This wouldst thou? Let it be!
Kneel down, and take the word divine,
ABSOLVO TE."

Off Cape St. Vincent. *December 14, 1832.*

MEMORY

MY home is now a thousand miles away;
Yet in my thoughts its every image fair
Rises as keen, as I still linger'd there,
And, turning me, could all I loved survey.
And so, upon Death's unaverted day,
As I speed upwards, I shall on me bear,
And in no breathless whirl, the things that were,
And duties given, and ends I did obey.
And, when at length I reach the Throne of Power,
Ah! still unscared, I shall in fulness see
The vision of my past innumerous deeds,
My deep heart-courses, and their motive-seeds,
So to gaze on till the red dooming hour.
Lord, in that strait, the Judge! remember me!

Off Cape Trafalgar. *December 15, 1832.*

THE HAVEN

WHENCE is this awe, by stillness spread
O'er the world-fretted soul?
Wave rear'd on wave its godless head,
While my keen bark, by breezes sped,
Dash'd fiercely through the ocean bed,
And chafed towards its goal.

But now there reigns so deep a rest,
That I could almost weep.
Sinner! thou hast in this rare guest
Of Adam's peace a figure blest;
'Tis Eden seen, though not possess'd,
Which cherub-flames still keep.

Gibraltar. *December 16, 1832.*

A WORD IN SEASON

O LORD! when sin's close-marshall'd line
Assails Thy witness on his way,
How should he raise Thy glorious sign,
And how Thy will display?

Thy holy Paul, with soul of flame,
Rose on Mars' hill, a soldier lone;
Shall I thus speak th' Atoning Name,
Though with a heart of stone?

"Not so," He said: "hush thee, and seek,
With thoughts in prayer and watchful eyes,
My seasons sent for thee to speak,
And use them as they rise."

Gibraltar. *December 17, 1832.*

FAIR WORDS

THY words are good, and freely given,
As though thou felt them true;
Friend, think thee well, to hell or heaven
A serious heart is due.

It pains thee sore, man's will should swerve
In his true path divine;
And yet thou ventur'st nought to serve
Thy neighbour's weal nor thine.

Beware! such words may once be said,
Where shame and fear unite;
But, spoken twice, they mark instead
A sin against the light.

Gibraltar. *December 17, 1832.*

ENGLAND

TYRE of the West, and glorying in the name
More than in Faith's pure fame!
O trust not crafty fort nor rock renown'd
Earn'd upon hostile ground;
Wielding Trade's master-keys, at thy proud will
To lock or loose its waters, England! trust not still.

Dread thine own power! Since haughty Babel's prime
High towers have been man's crime.
Since her hoar age, when the huge moat lay bare,
Strongholds have been man's snare.
Thy nest is in the crags; ah! refuge frail!
Mad counsel in its hour, or traitors, will prevail.

He who scann'd Sodom for His righteous men
Still spares thee for thy ten;
But, should vain tongues the Bride of Heaven defy,
He will not pass thee by;
For, as earth's kings welcome their spotless guest,
So gives He them by turn, to suffer or be blest.

At sea. *December 18, 1832.*

MOSES

MOSES, the patriot fierce, became
The meekest man on earth,
To show us how love's quick'ning flame
Can give our souls new birth.

Moses, the man of meekest heart,
Lost Canaan by self-will,
To show, where Grace has done its part,
How sin defiles us still.

Thou, who hast taught me in Thy fear,
Yet seest me frail at best,
O grant me loss with Moses here,
To gain his future rest!

At Sea. *December 19, 1832.*

THE PATIENT CHURCH

BIDE thou thy time!
Watch with meek eyes the race of pride and crime,
Sit in the gate, and be the heathen's jest,
Smiling and self-possest.
O thou, to whom is pledged a victor's sway,
Bide thou the victor's day!

Think on the sin[1]
That reap'd the unripe seed, and toil'd to win
Foul history-marks at Bethel and at Dan;
No blessing, but a ban;
Whilst the wise Shepherd[2] hid his heaven-told fate,
Nor reck'd a tyrant's hate.

Such loss is gain;
Wait the bright Advent that shall loose thy chain!
E'en now the shadows break, and gleams divine
Edge the dim distant line.
When thrones are trembling, and earth's fat ones quail,
True Seed! thou shalt prevail!

Off Algiers. *December 20, 1832.*

[1] Jeroboam.

[2] David.

JEREMIAH

"Oh that I had in the wilderness a lodging-place of wayfaring men; that I might leave my people, and go from them!"

"WOE'S me! the peaceful prophet cried,
"Spare me this troubled life;
To stem man's wrath, to school his pride,
To head the sacred strife!

"O place me in some silent vale,
Where groves and flowers abound;
Nor eyes that grudge, nor tongues that rail,
Vex the truth-haunted ground!"

If his meek spirit err'd, opprest,
That God denied repose,
What sin is ours, to whom Heaven's rest
Is pledged, to heal earth's woes?

Off Galita. *December 22, 1832.*

PENANCE

MORTAL! if e'er thy spirits faint,
By grief or pain opprest,
Seek not vain hope, or sour complaint,
To cheer or ease thy breast:

But view thy bitterest pangs as sent
A shadow of that doom,
Which is the soul's just punishment
In its own guilt's true home.

Be thine own judge; hate thy proud heart;
And while the sad drops flow,
E'en let thy will attend the smart,
And sanctify thy woe.

Off Pantellaria. *December 23, 1832.*

THE COURSE OF TRUTH

Him God raised up the third day, and shewed Him openly,
not to all the people, but unto witnesses chosen before of God.

WHEN royal Truth, released from mortal throes,
Burst His brief slumber, and triumphant rose,
Ill had the Holiest sued
A patron multitude,
Or courted Tetrach's eye, or claim'd to rule
By the world's winning grace, or proofs from learned school.

But, robing Him in viewless air, He told
His secret to a few of meanest mould;
They in their turn imparted
The gift to men pure-hearted,
While the brute many heard His mysteries high,
As some strange fearful tongue, and crouch'd, they knew not why.

Still is the might of Truth, as it has been:
Lodged in the few, obey'd, and yet unseen.
Rear'd on lone heights, and rare,
His saints their watch-flame bear,
And the mad world sees the wide-circling blaze,
Vain searching whence it streams, and how to quench its rays.

Malta. *December 24, 1832.*

CHRISTMAS WITHOUT CHRIST

HOW can I keep my Christmas feast
In its due festive show,
Reft of the sight of the High Priest
From whom its glories flow?

I hear the tuneful bells around,
The blessed towers I see;
A stranger on a foreign ground,
They peal a fast for me.

O Britons! now so brave and high,
How will ye weep the day
When Christ in judgment passes by,
And calls the Bride away!

Your Christmas then will lose its mirth,
  Your Easter lose its bloom:
Abroad, a scene of strife and dearth;
  Within, a cheerless home!

Malta. *December 25, 1832.*

SLEEPLESSNESS

UNWEARIED God, before whose face
  The night is clear as day,
Whilst we, poor worms, o'er life's scant race
  Now creep, and now delay,
We with death's foretaste alternate
Our labour's dint and sorrow's weight,
Save in that fever-troubled state
  Where pain or care has sway.

Dread Lord! Thy glory, watchfulness,
  Is but disease in man;
We to our cost our bounds transgress
  In Thy eternal plan:
Pride grasps the powers by Thee display'd,
Yet ne'er the rebel effort made
But fell beneath the sudden shade
  Of nature's withering ban.

Malta. *December 26, 1832.*

ABRAHAM

THE better portion didst thou choose, Great Heart,
Thy God's first choice, and pledge of Gentile grace!
  Faith's truest type, he with unruffled face
Bore the world's smile, and bade her slaves depart;
Whether, a trader, with no trader's art,
  He buys in Canaan his last resting-place,—
  Or freely yields rich Siddim's ample space,—
Or braves the rescue, and the battle's smart,
Yet scorns the heathen gifts of those he saved.
O happy in their soul's high solitude,
Who commune thus with God, and not with earth!
Amid the scoffings of the wealth-enslaved,
A ready prey, as though in absent mood
They calmly move, nor reck the unmanner'd mirth.

At Sea. *December 27, 1832.*

THE GREEK FATHERS

LET heathens sing thy heathen praise,
Fall'n Greece! the thought of holier days
In my sad heart abides;
For sons of Thine in Truth's first hour
Were tongues and weapons of His power,
Born of the Spirit's fiery shower,
Our fathers and our guides.

All thine is Clement's varied page;
And Dionysius, ruler sage,
In days of doubt and pain;
And Origen with eagle eye;
And saintly Basil's purpose high
To smite imperial heresy,
And cleanse the Altar's stain.

From thee the glorious preacher came,
With soul of zeal and lips of flame,
A court's stern martyr-guest;
And thine, O inexhaustive race!
Was Nazianzen's heaven-taught grace;
And royal-hearted Athanase,
With Paul's own mantle blest.

Off Zante. *December 28, 1832.*

THE WITNESS

HOW shall a child of God fulfil
His vow to cleanse his soul from ill,
And raise on high his baptism-light,
Like Aaron's seed in vestment white,
And holy-hearted Nazarite?

First, let him shun the haunts of vice,
Sin-feast, or heathen sacrifice;
Fearing the board of wealthy pride,
Or heretic, self-trusting guide,
Or where the adulterer's smiles preside.

Next, as he threads the maze of men,
Aye must he lift his witness, when
A sin is spoke in Heaven's dread face,
And none at hand of higher grace
The Cross to carry in his place.

But if he hears and sits him still,
First, he will lose his hate of ill;
Next, fear of sinning, after hate;
Small sins his heart then desecrate;
And last, despair persuades to great.

Off Ithaca. *December* 30, 1832.

THE DEATH OF MOSES

MY Father's hope! my childhood's dream!
The promise from on high!
Long waited for! its glories beam
Now when my death is nigh.

My death is come, but not decay;
Nor eye nor mind is dim;
The keenness of youth's vigorous day
Thrills in each nerve and limb.

Blest scene! thrice welcome after toil—
If no deceit I view;
O might my lips but press the soil,
And prove the vision true!

Its glorious heights, its wealthy plains,
Its many-tinted groves,
They call! but He my steps restrains
Who chastens whom He loves.

Ah! now they melt...they are but shades...
I die!—yet is no rest,
O Lord! in store, since Canaan fades
But seen, and not possest?

Off Ithaca. *December* 30, 1832.

CORCYRA

I SAT beneath an olive's branches grey,
And gazed upon the site of a lost town,
By sage and poet raised to long renown;
Where dwelt a race that on the sea held sway,
And, restless as its waters, forced a way
For civil strife a hundred states to drown.
That multitudinous stream we now note down
As though one life, in birth and in decay.
But is their being's history spent and run,
Whose spirits live in awful singleness,
Each in its self-form'd sphere of light or gloom?
Henceforth, while pondering the fierce deeds then done,
Such reverence on me shall its seal impress
As though I corpses saw, and walk'd the tomb.

At Sea. *January 7, 1833.*

MELCHIZEDEK

Without father, without mother, without descent; having neither beginning of days, nor end of life.

THRICE bless'd are they, who feel their loneliness;
To whom nor voice of friends nor pleasant scene
Brings aught on which the sadden'd heart can lean;
Yea, the rich earth, garb'd in her daintiest dress
Of light and joy, doth but the more oppress,
Claiming responsive smiles and rapture high;
Till, sick at heart, beyond the veil they fly,
Seeking His Presence, who alone can bless.
Such, in strange days, the weapons of Heaven's grace;
When, passing o'er the high-born Hebrew line,
He moulds the vessel of His vast design;
Fatherless, homeless, reft of age and place,
Sever'd from earth, and careless of its wreck,
Born through long woe His rare Melchizedek.

Corfu. *January* 5, 1833.

TRANSFIGURATION

They glorified God in me.

I SAW thee once, and nought discern'd
For stranger to admire;
A serious aspect, but it burn'd
With no unearthly fire.

Again I saw, and I confess'd
Thy speech was rare and high;
And yet it vex'd my burden'd breast,
And scared, I knew not why.

I saw once more, and awe-struck gazed
On face, and form, and air;
God's living glory round thee blazed—
A Saint—a Saint was there!

Off Zante. *January* 8, 1833.

BEHIND THE VEIL

BANISH'D the House of sacred rest,
Amid a thoughtless throng,
At length I heard its creed confess'd,
And knelt the saints among.

Artless his strain and unadorn'd,
Who spoke Christ's message there;
But what at home I might have scorn'd,
Now charm'd my famish'd ear.

Lord, grant me this abiding grace,
Thy Word and sons to know;
To pierce the veil on Moses' face,
Although his speech be slow.

At Sea. *January 9, 1833.*

JUDGMENT

IF e'er I fall beneath Thy rod,
As through life's snares I go,
Save me from David's lot, O God!
And choose Thyself the woe.

How should I face Thy plagues? which scare,
And haunt, and stun, until
The heart or sinks in mute despair,
Or names a random ill.

If else...then guide in David's path,
Who chose the holier pain;
Satan and man are tools of wrath,
An Angel's scourge is gain.

Off Malta. *January 10, 1833.*

SENSITIVENESS

TIME was, I shrank from what was right
From fear of what was wrong;
I would not brave the sacred fight,
Because the foe was strong.

But now I cast that finer sense
  And sorer shame aside;
Such dread of sin was indolence,
  Such aim at Heaven was pride.

So, when my Saviour calls, I rise
  And calmly do my best;
Leaving to Him, with silent eyes
  Of hope and fear, the rest.

I step, I mount where He has led;
  Men count my haltings o'er;—
I know them; yet, though self I dread,
  I love His precept more.

Lazaret, Malta. *January 15, 1833.*

DAVID AND JONATHAN

Thy love to me was wonderful, passing the love of women.

O HEART of fire! misjudged by wilful man,
  Thou flower of Jesse's race!
What woe was thine, when thou and Jonathan
  Last greeted face to face!
He doom'd to die, thou on us to impress
The portent of a blood-stain'd holiness.

Yet it was well:—for so, 'mid cares of rule
  And crime's encircling tide,
A spell was o'er thee, zealous one, to cool
  Earth-joy and kingly pride;
With battle-scene and pageant, prompt to blend
The pale calm spectre of a blameless friend.

Ah! had he lived, before thy throne to stand,
  Thy spirit keen and high
Sure it had snapp'd in twain love's slender band,
  So dear in memory;
Paul, of his comrade reft, the warning gives,—
He lives to us who dies, he is but lost who lives.

Lazaret, Malta. *January 16, 1833.*

HUMILIATION

I HAVE been honour'd and obey'd,
I have met scorn and slight;
And my heart loves earth's sober shade,
More than her laughing light.

For what is rule but a sad weight
Of duty and a snare?
What meanness, but with happier fate
The Saviour's Cross to share?

This my hid choice, if not from heaven,
Moves on the heavenward line;
Cleanse it, good Lord, from earthly leaven,
And make it simply Thine.

Lazaret, Malta. *January 16, 1833.*

THE CALL OF DAVID

And the Lord said, Arise, anoint him, for this is he.

LATEST born of Jesse's race,
Wonder lights thy bashful face,
While the Prophet's gifted oil
Seals thee for a path of toil.
We, thy Angels, circling round thee,
Ne'er shall find thee as we found thee,
When thy faith first brought us near
In thy lion-fight severe.

Go! and mid thy flocks awhile
At thy doom of greatness smile;
Bold to bear God's heaviest load,
Dimly guessing of the road,—
Rocky road, and scarce ascended,
Though thy foot be angel-tended.

Twofold praise thou shalt attain,
In royal court and battle plain;
Then comes heart-ache, care, distress,
Blighted hope, and loneliness;
Wounds from friend and gifts from foe,
Dizzied faith, and guilt, and woe;

Loftiest aims by earth defiled,
Gleams of wisdom sin-beguiled,
Sated power's tyrannic mood,
Counsels shared with men of blood,
Sad success, parental tears,
And a dreary gift of years.

Strange, that guileless face and form
To lavish on the scarring storm!
Yet we take thee in thy blindness,
And we buffet thee in kindness;
Little chary of thy fame,—
Dust unborn may bless or blame,—
But we mould thee for the root
Of man's promised healing Fruit,
And we mould thee hence to rise,
As our brother, to the skies.

Lazaret, Malta. *January 18, 1833.*

A BLIGHT

WHAT time by heart unfolded its fresh leaves
In springtime gay, and scatter'd flowers around,
A whisper warn'd of earth's unhealthy ground,
And all that there love's light and pureness grieves;
Sun's ray and canker-worm
And sudden-whelming storm;—
But, ah! my self-will smiled, nor reck'd the gracious sound.

So now defilement dims life's memory-springs;
I cannot hear an early-cherish'd strain,
But first a joy, and then it brings a pain—
Fear, and self-hate, and vain remorseful stings:
Tears lull my grief to rest,
Not without hope, this breast
May one day lose its load, and youth yet bloom again.

Lazaret, Malta. *January 19, 1833.*

JOSEPH

O PUREST Symbol of the Eternal Son!
Who dwelt in thee, as in some sacred shrine,
To draw hearts after thee, and make them thine;
Not parent only by that light was won,
And brethren crouch'd who had in wrath begun,
But heathen pomp abased her at the sign
And the hid Presence of a guest divine,
Till a king heard, and all thou bad'st was done.
Then was fulfill'd Nature's dim augury,
That "Wisdom, clad in visible form, would be
So fair, that all must love and bow the knee;"
Lest it might seem, what time the Substance came,
Truth lack'd a sceptre, when It but laid by
Its beaming front, and bore a willing shame.

Lazaret, Malta. *January 20, 1833.*

ISAAC

MANY the guileless years the Patriarch spent,
Bless'd in the wife a father's foresight chose;
Many the prayers and gracious deeds, which rose
Daily thank-offerings from his pilgrim tent.
Yet these, though written in the heavens, are rent
From out truth's lower roll, which sternly shows
But one sad trespass at his history's close,
Father's, son's, mother's, and its punishment.
Not in their brightness, but their earthly stains
Are the true seed vouchsafed to earthly eyes.
Sin can read sin, but dimly scans high grace,
So we move heavenward with averted face,
Scared into faith by warning of sin's pains;
And Saints are lower'd, that the world may rise.

Valletta. *January 23, 1833.*

REVERSES

WHEN mirth is full and free,
Some sudden gloom shall be;
When haughty power mounts high,
The Watcher's axe is nigh.
All growth has bound; when greatest found,
  It hastes to die.

When the rich town, that long
Has lain its huts among,
Uprears its pageants vast,
And vaunts—it shall not last!
Bright tints that shine, are but a sign
  Of summer past.

And when thine eye surveys,
With fond adoring gaze,
And yearning heart, thy friend—
Love to its grave doth tend.
All gifts below, save Truth, but grow
  Towards an end.

Valletta. *January 30, 1833.*

HOPE

WE are not children of a guilty sire,
Since Noe stepp'd from out his wave-toss'd home,
  And a stern baptism flush'd earth's faded bloom.
Not that the heavens then clear'd, or cherub's fire
From Eden's portal did at once retire;
  But thoughts were stirr'd of Him who was to come,
  Whose rainbow hues so streak'd the o'ershadowing gloom,
That faith could e'en that desolate scene admire.
The Lord has come and gone; and now we wait
The second substance of the deluge type,
When our slight ark shall cross a molten surge;
So, while the gross earth melts, for judgment ripe,
Ne'er with its haughty turrets to emerge,
We shall mount up to Eden's long-lost gate.

Valletta. *February 5, 1833.*

ST. PAUL AT MELITA

And when Paul had gathered a bundle of sticks, and laid them on the fire, there came a viper out of the heat.

SECURE in his prophetic strength,
 The water peril o'er,
The many-gifted man at length
 Stepp'd on the promised shore.

He trod the shore; but not to rest,
 Nor wait till Angels came;
Lo! humblest pains the Saint attest,
 The firebrands and the flame.

But, when he felt the viper's smart,
 Then instant aid was given;
Christian! hence learn to do thy part,
 And leave the rest to Heaven.

Messina. *February* 9, 1833.

MESSINA

Homo sum; humani nil a me alienum puto.

WHY, wedded to the Lord, still yearns my heart
Towards these scenes of ancient heathen fame?
  Yet legend hoar, and voice of bard that came
Fixing my restless youth with its sweet art,
And shades of power, and those who bore a part
  In the mad deeds that set the world on flame,
  So fret my memory here,—ah! is it blame?—
That from my eyes the tear is fain to start.
Nay, from no fount impure these drops arise;
'Tis but that sympathy with Adam's race
Which in each brother's history reads its own.
So let the cliffs and seas of this fair place
Be named man's tomb and splendid record-stone,
High hope, pride-stain'd, the course without the prize.

Messina. *February* 9, 1833.

WARNINGS

WHEN Heaven sends sorrow,
  Warnings go first,
  Lest it should burst
  With stunning might
  On souls too bright
    To fear the morrow.

Can science bear us
  To the hid springs
  Of human things?
  Why may not dream,
  Or thought's day-gleam,
    Startle, yet cheer us?

Are such thoughts fetters,
  While Faith disowns
  Dread of earth's tones,
  Recks but Heaven's call,
  And on the wall
    Reads but Heaven's letters?

Between Calatafimi and Palermo. *February 12*, 1833.

DREAMS

OH! miserable power
To dreams allow'd, to raise the guilty past,
And back awhile the illumined spirit to cast
On its youth's twilight hour;
In mockery guiling it to act again
The revel or the scoff in Satan's frantic train!

Nay, hush thee, angry heart!
An Angel's grief ill fits a penitent;
Welcome the thorn—it is divinely sent,
And with its wholesome smart
Shall pierce thee in thy virtue's palmy home,
And warn thee what thou art, and whence thy
wealth has come.

Paestum. *February 26, 1833.*

TEMPTATION

O HOLY Lord, who with the Children Three
Didst walk the piercing flame,
Help, in those trial-hours, which, save to Thee,
I dare not name;
Nor let these quivering eyes and sickening heart
Crumble to dust beneath the Tempter's dart.

Thou, who didst once Thy life from Mary's breast
Renew from day to day,
Oh, might her smile, severely sweet, but rest
On this frail clay!
Till I am Thine with my whole soul; and fear,
Not feel a secret joy, that Hell is near.

Frascati. *March 28, 1833.*

OUR FUTURE

What I do, thou knowest not now; but thou shalt know hereafter.

DID we but see,
When life first open'd, how our journey lay
Between its earliest and its closing day,
Or view ourselves, as we one time shall be,
Who strive for the high prize, such sight would break
The youthful spirit, though bold for Jesu's sake.

But Thou, dear Lord!
Whilst I traced out bright scenes which were to come,
Isaac's pure blessings, and a verdant home,
Didst spare me, and withhold Thy fearful word;
Wiling me year by year, till I am found
A pilgrim pale, with Paul's sad girdle bound.

Tre Fontane. *April 2, 1833.*

HEATHENISM

'MID Balak's magic fires
The Spirit spake, clear as in Israel;
With prayers untrue and covetous desires
Did God vouchsafe to dwell;
Who summon'd dreams, His earlier word to bring
To patient Job's vex'd friends, and Gerar's guileless king.

If such o'erflowing grace
From Aaron's vest e'en on the Sibyl ran,
Why should we fear, the Son now lacks His place
Where roams unchristen'd man?
As though, when faith is keen, He cannot make
Bread of the very stones, or thirst with ashes slake.

Messina. *April 21, 1833.*

TAORMINI

And Jacob went on his way, and the Angels of God met him.

SAY, hast thou track'd a traveller's round,
Nor visions met thee there,
Thou couldst but marvel to have found
This blighted world so fair?

And feel an awe within thee rise,
    That sinful man should see
Glories far worthier Seraph's eyes
    Than to be shared by thee?

Store them in heart! thou shalt not faint
    'Mid coming pains and fears,
As the third heaven once nerved a Saint
    For fourteen trial-years.

Magnisi. *April 26, 1833.*

RELICS OF SAINTS

He is not the God of the dead, but of the living;
for all live unto Him.

"THE Fathers are in dust, yet live to God:"—
  So says the Truth; as if the motionless clay
Still held the seeds of life beneath the sod,
  Smouldering and struggling till the judgment-day.

And hence we learn with reverence to esteem
  Of these frail houses, though the grave confines;
Sophist may urge his cunning tests, and deem
  That they are earth;—but they are heavenly shrines.

Palermo. *June 1, 1833.*

DAY-LABOURERS

And He said, It is finished.

ONE Only, of God's messengers to man,
Finish'd the work of grace, which He began;
E'en Moses wearied upon Nebo's height,
    Though loth to leave the fight
With the doom'd foe, and yield the sun-bright land
    To Joshua's armèd hand.

And David wrought in turn a strenuous part,
Zeal for God's house consuming him in heart;
And yet he might not build, but only bring
    Gifts for the Heavenly King;
And these another rear'd, his peaceful son,
    Till the full work was done.

List, Christian warrior! thou, whose soul is fain
To rid thy Mother of her present chain;—
Christ will avenge His Bride; yea, even now
Begins the work, and thou
Shalt spend in it thy strength, but, ere He save,
Thy lot shall be the grave.

Palermo. *June 2, 1833.*

WARFARE

Freely ye have received; freely give.

"GIVE any boon for peace!
Why should our fair-eyed Mother e'er engage
In the world's course and on a troubled stage,
From which her very call is a release?
No! in thy garden stand,
And tend with pious hand
The flowers thou plantest there,
Which are thy proper care,
O man of God! in meekness and in love,
And waiting for the blissful realms above."

Alas! for thou must learn,
Thou guileless one! rough is the holy hand;
Runs not the Word of Truth through every land,
A sword to sever, and a fire to burn?
If blessèd Paul had stay'd
In cot or learned shade,
With the priest's white attire,
And the Saints' tuneful choir,
Men had not gnash'd their teeth, nor risen to slay,
But thou hadst been a heathen in thy day.

Palermo. *June 3, 1833.*

SACRILEGE

THE Church shone brightly in her youthful days,
Ere the world on her smiled;
So now, an outcast, she would pour her rays
Keen, free and undefiled:
Yet would I not that arm of force were mine,
Which thrusts her from her awful ancient shrine.

'Twas duty bound each convert-king to rear
His Mother from the dust,
And pious was it to enrich, nor fear
Christ for the rest to trust;
And who shall dare make common or unclean
What once has on the Holy Altar been?

Dear brothers!—hence, while ye for ill prepare,
Triumph is still your own;
Blest is a pilgrim Church!—yet shrink to share
The curse of throwing down.
So will we toil in our old place to stand,
Watching, not dreading, the despoiler's hand.

Palermo. *June 4, 1833.*

LIBERALISM

Jehu destroyed Baal out of Israel. Howbeit from the sins of Jeroboam Jehu departed not from after them, to wit, the golden calves that were in Bethel, and that were in Dan.

YE cannot halve the Gospel of God's grace;
Men of presumptuous heart! I know you well.
Ye are of those who plan that we should dwell,
Each in his tranquil home and holy place;
Seeing the Word refines all natures rude,
And tames the stirrings of the multitude.

And ye have caught some echoes of its lore,
As heralded amid the joyous choirs;
Ye mark'd it spoke of peace, chastised desires,
Good-will and mercy,—and ye heard no more;
But, as for zeal and quick-eyed sanctity,
And the dread depths of grace, ye pass'd them by.

And so ye halve the Truth; for ye in heart,
At best, are doubters whether it be true,
The theme discarding, as unmeet for you,
Statesmen or Sages. O new-encompass'd art
Of the ancient Foe!—but what, if it extends
O'er our own camp, and rules amid our friends?

Palermo. *June 5, 1833.*

DECLENSION

WHEN I am sad, I say,
"What boots it me to strive,
And vex my spirit day by day,
Dead memories to revive?

"Alas! what good will come,
Though we our prayer obtain,
To bring old times triumphant home,
And wandering flocks regain?

"Would not our history run
In the same weary round,
And service in meek faith begun,
At length in forms be bound?

"Union would give us strength—
That strength the earth subdue;
And then comes wealth, and pride at length,
And sloth, and prayers untrue."

Nay, this is worldly-wise;
To reason is a crime,
Since the Lord bade His Church arise,
In the dark ancient time.

He wills that she should shine;
So we her flame must trim
Around His soul-converting Sign,
And leave the rest to Him.

Palermo. *June 6, 1833.*

THE AGE TO COME

WHEN I would search the truths that in me burn,
And mould them into rule and argument,
A hundred reasoners cried,—"Hast thou to learn
Those dreams are scatter'd now, those fires are spent?"
And, did I mount to simpler thoughts, and try
Some theme of peace, 'twas still the same reply.

Perplex'd, I hoped my heart was pure of guile,
  But judged me weak in wit, to disagree;
But now, I see that men are mad awhile,
  And joy the Age to come will think with me:—
'Tis the old history—Truth without a home,
Despised and slain, then rising from the tomb.

Palermo. *June 9, 1833.*

EXTERNAL RELIGION

WHEN first earth's rulers welcomed home
  The Church, their zeal impress'd
Upon the seasons, as they come,
  The image of their guest.

Men's words and works, their hopes and fears,
  Henceforth forbid to rove,
Paused, when a Martyr claim'd her tears,
  Or Saint inspired her love.

But craving wealth, and feverish power,
  Such service now discard;
The loss of one excited hour
  A sacrifice too hard!

And e'en about the holiest day,
  God's own in every time,
They doubt and search, lest aught should stay
  A cataract of crime.

Where shall this cease? must crosiers fall,
  Shrines suffer touch profane,
Till, cast without His vineyard wall,
  The Heaven-sent Heir is slain?

Palermo. *June 11, 1833.*

ST. GREGORY NAZIANZEN

PEACE-LOVING man, of humble heart and true!
What dost thou here?
Fierce is the city's crowd; the lordly few
Are dull of ear!
Sore pain it was to thee,—till thou didst quit
Thy patriarch-throne at length, as though for power unfit.

So works the All-wise! our services dividing
Not as we ask:
For the world's profit, by our gifts deciding
Our duty-task.
See in king's courts loth Jeremias plead;
And slow-tongued Moses rule by eloquence of deed!

Yes! thou, bright Angel of the East! didst rear
The Cross divine,
Borne high upon thy liquid accents, where
Men mock'd the Sign;
Till that cold city heard thy battle-cry,
And hearts were stirr'd, and deem'd a Pentecost was nigh.

Thou couldst a people raise, but couldst not rule:—
So, gentle one,
Heaven set thee free,—for, ere thy years were full,
Thy work was done;
According thee the lot thou lovedst best,
To muse upon the past,—to serve, yet be at rest.

Palermo. *June 12, 1833.*

THE GOOD SAMARITAN

O THAT thy creed were sound[1]!
For thou dost soothe the heart, thou Church of Rome,
By thy unwearied watch and varied round
Of service, in thy Saviour's holy home.
I cannot walk the city's sultry streets,
But the wide porch invites to still retreats,
Where passion's thirst is calm'd, and care's unthankful gloom.

There, on a foreign shore,
The homesick solitary finds a friend:
Thoughts, prison'd long for lack of speech, outpour
Their tears, and doubts in resignation end.
I almost fainted from the long delay
That tangles me within this languid bay,
When comes a foe, my wounds with oil and wine to tend.

Palermo. *June 13, 1833.*

[1] Of course this is the exclamation of one who was not in Catholic Communion.

THE PILLAR OF THE CLOUD

LEAD, Kindly Light, amid the encircling gloom,
Lead Thou me on!
The night is dark, and I am far from home—
Lead Thou me on!
Keep Thou my feet; I do not ask to see
The distant scene—one step enough for me.

I was not ever thus, nor pray'd that Thou
Shouldst lead me on.
I loved to choose and see my path, but now
Lead Thou me on!
I loved the garish day, and, spite of fears,
Pride ruled my will: remember not past years.

So long Thy power hath blest me, sure it still
Will lead me on,
O'er moor and fen, o'er crag and torrent, till
The night is gone;
And with the morn those angel faces smile
Which I have loved long since, and lost awhile.

At Sea. *June 16, 1833.*

JONAH

But Jonah rose up to flee unto Tarshish, from the presence of the Lord.

DEEP in his meditative bower,
  The tranquil seer reclined;
Numbering the creepers of an hour,
  The gourds which o'er him twined.

To note each plant, to rear each fruit
  Which soothes the languid sense,
He deem'd a safe, refined pursuit,—
  His Lord, an indolence.

The sudden voice was heard at length,
  "Lift thou the prophet's rod!"
But sloth had sapp'd the prophet's strength,
  He fear'd, and fled from God.

Next, by a fearful judgment tamed,
  He threats the offending race;
God spares;—he murmurs, pride-inflamed,
  His threat made void by grace.

What?—pride and sloth! man's worst of foes!
  And can such guests invade
Our choicest bliss, the green repose
  Of the sweet garden-shade?

Off Sardinia. *June 18, 1833.*

FAITH AGAINST SIGHT

As it was in the days of Lot, so shall it be also in the day of the Son of Man.

THE world has cycles in its course, when all
That once has been, is acted o'er again:—
Not by some fated law, which need appal
Our faith, or binds our deeds as with a chain;
But by men's separate sins, which blended still
The same bad round fulfil.

Then fear ye not, though Gallio's scorn ye see,
And soft-clad nobles count you mad, true hearts!
These are the fig-tree's signs;—rough deeds must be,
Trials and crimes: so learn ye well your parts.
Once more to plough the earth it is decreed,
And scatter wide the seed.

Off Sardinia. *June 18, 1833.*

DESOLATION

O SAY not thou art left of God,
Because His tokens in the sky
Thou canst not read: this earth He trod
To teach thee He was ever nigh.

He sees, beneath the fig-tree green,
Nathaniel con His sacred lore;
Shouldst thou thy chamber seek, unseen,
He enters through the unopen'd door.

And when thou liest, by slumber bound,
Outwearied in the Christian fight,
In glory, girt with Saints around,
He stands above thee through the night.

When friends to Emmaus bend their course
He joins, although He holds their eyes:
Or, shouldst thou feel some fever's force,
He takes thy hand, He bids thee rise.

Or on a voyage, when calms prevail,
And prison thee upon the sea,
He walks the wave, He wings the sail,
The shore is gain'd, and thou art free.

Off Sardinia. *June 18, 1833.*

ZEAL AND PATIENCE

I, Paul, the prisoner of the Lord.

O COMRADE bold of toil and pain!
Thy trial how severe,
When sever'd first by prisoner's chain
From thy loved labour-sphere!

Say, did impatience first impel
The heaven-sent bond to break?
Or, couldst thou bear its hindrance well,
Loitering for Jesu's sake?

Oh, might we know! for sore we feel
The languor of delay,
When sickness lets our fainter zeal,
Or foes block up our way.

Lord! who Thy thousand years dost wait
To work the thousandth part
Of Thy vast plan, for us create
With zeal a patient heart.

Off Sardinia. *June 19, 1833.*

THE RELIGION OF CAIN

Am I my brother's keeper?

THE time has been, it seem'd a precept plain
Of the true faith, Christ's tokens to display;
And in life's commerce still the thought retain,
That men have souls, and wait a judgment-day;
Kings used their gifts as ministers of heaven,
Nor stripp'd their zeal for God, of means which God had given.

'Tis alter'd now;—for Adam's eldest born
  Has train'd our practice in a selfish rule,
Each stands alone, Christ's bonds asunder torn;
  Each has his private thought, selects his school,
  Conceals his creed, and lives in closest tie
Of fellowship with those who count it blasphemy.

Brothers! spare reasoning;—men have settled long
  That ye are out of date, and they are wise;
Use their own weapons; let your words be strong,
  Your cry be loud, till each scared boaster flies;
  Thus the Apostles tamed the pagan breast,
They argued not, but preach'd; and conscience did the rest.

Off Sardinia. *June 19, 1833.*

ST. PAUL

I DREAM'D that, with a passionate complaint,
  I wish'd me born amid God's deeds of might;
  And envied those who had the presence bright
Of gifted Prophet and strong-hearted Saint,
Whom my heart loves, and Fancy strives to paint.
  I turn'd, when straight a stranger met my sight,
  Came as my guest, and did awhile unite
His lot with mine, and lived without restraint.
Courteous he was, and grave,—so meek in mien,
It seem'd untrue, or told a purpose weak;
Yet, in the mood, he could with aptness speak,
Or with stern force, or show of feelings keen,
Marking deep craft, methought, or hidden pride:—
Then came a voice,—"St. Paul is at thy side."

Off Sardinia. *June 20, 1833.*

FLOWERS WITHOUT FRUIT

PRUNE thou thy words, the thoughts control
  That o'er thee swell and throng;
They will condense within thy soul,
  And change to purpose strong.

But he who lets his feelings run
  In soft luxurious flow,
Shrinks when hard service must be done,
  And faints at every woe.

Faith's meanest deed more favour bears,
  Where hearts and wills are weigh'd,
Than brightest transports, choicest prayers,
  Which bloom their hour and fade.

Off Sardinia. *June* 20, 1833.

ZEAL AND MEEKNESS

CHRIST bade his followers take the sword;
  And yet He chid the deed,
When hasty Peter seized His word,
  And made a foe to bleed.

The gospel Creed, a sword of strife,
  Meek hands alone may rear;
And ever Zeal begins its life
  In silent thought and fear.

Ye, who would weed the Vineyard's soil,
  Treasure the lesson given;
Lest in the judgment-books ye toil
  For Satan, not for heaven.

Off Sardinia. *June* 20, 1833.

VEXATIONS

EACH trial has its weight; which, whoso bears
Knows his own woe, and need of succouring grace;
  The martyr's hope half wipes away the trace
Of flowing blood; the while life's humblest cares
Smart more, because they hold in Holy Writ no place.

This be my comfort, in these days of grief,
  Which is not Christ's, nor forms heroic tale.
  Apart from Him, if not a sparrow fail,
May not He pitying view, and send relief
When foes or friends perplex, and peevish thoughts prevail?

Then keep good heart, nor take the niggard course
  Of Thomas, who must see ere he would trust.
  Faith will fill up God's word, not poorly just
To the bare letter, heedless of its force,
But walking by its light amid earth's sun and dust.

Off Sardinia. *June 21, 1833.*

THE CHURCH IN PRAYER

WHY loiterest within Simon's walls,
  Hard by the barren sea,
Thou Saint! when many a sinner calls
  To preach and set him free?

Can this be he, who erst confess'd
  For Christ affection keen,
Now truant in untimely rest,
  The mood of an Essene?

Yet he who at the sixth hour sought
  The lone house-top to pray,
There gain'd a sight beyond his thought,
  The dawn of Gentile day.

Then reckon not, when perils lour,
  The time of prayer mis-spent;
Nor meanest chance, nor place, nor hour,
  Without its heavenward bent.

Off Sardinia. *June 21, 1833.*

THE WRATH TO COME

From His mouth came out a sharp two-edged sword.

WHEN first God stirr'd me, and the Church's word
  Came as a theme of reverent search and fear,
  It little cost to own the lustre clear
O'er rule she taught, and rite, and rule she stored;
For conscience craved, and reason did accord.
  Yet one there was that wore a mien austere,
  And I did doubt, and, troubled, ask'd to hear
Whose mouth had force to edge so sharp a sword.

My mother oped her trust, the holy Book;
And heal'd my pang. She pointed, and I found
Christ on Himself, considerate Master, took
The utterance of that doctrine's fearful sound.
The Fount of Love His servants sends to tell
Love's deeds; Himself reveals the sinner's hell.

Off Sardinia. *June 21, 1833.*

PUSILLANIMITY

I have need to be baptized of Thee, and comest Thou to me?

HOW didst thou start, Thou Holy Baptist, bid
To pour repentance on the Sinless Brow!
Then all thy meekness, from thy hearers hid
Beneath the Ascetic's port and Preacher's fire,
Flow'd forth, and with a pang thou didst desire
He might be chief, not thou.

And so on us at whiles it falls, to claim
Powers that we dread, or dare some forward part;
Nor must we shrink as cravens from the blame
Of pride, in common eyes, or purpose deep;
But with pure thoughts look up to God, and keep
Our secret in our heart.

At Sea. *June 22, 1833.*

JAMES AND JOHN

TWO brothers freely cast their lot
With David's royal Son;
The cost of conquest counting not,
They deem the battle won.

Brothers in heart, they hope to gain
An undivided joy;
That man may one with man remain,
As boy was one with boy.

Christ heard; and will'd that James should fall,
First prey of Satan's rage;
John linger out his fellows all,
And die in bloodless age.

Now they join hands once more above,
  Before the Conqueror's throne;
Thus God grants prayer, but in His love
  Makes times and ways His own.

At Sea. *June 22, 1833.*

HORA NOVISSIMA

WHENE'ER goes forth Thy dread command,
  And my last hour is nigh,
Lord, grant me in a Christian land,
  As I was born, to die.

I pray not, Lord, that friends may be,
  Or kindred, standing by,—
Choice blessing! which I leave to Thee
  To grant me or deny.

But let my failing limbs beneath
  My Mother's smile recline;
And prayers sustain my labouring breath
  From out her sacred shrine.

And let the cross beside my bed
  In its dread Presence rest;
And let the absolving words be said,
  To ease a laden breast.

Thou, Lord, where'er we lie, canst aid;
  But He, who taught His own
To live as one, will not upbraid
  The dread to die alone.

At Sea. *June 22, 1833.*

PROGRESS OF UNBELIEF

NOW is the Autumn of the Tree of Life;
Its leaves are shed upon the unthankful earth,
Which lets them whirl, a prey to the winds' strife,
Heartless to store them for the months of dearth.
Men close the door, and dress the cheerful hearth,
Self-trusting still; and in his comely gear
Of precept and of rite, a household Baal rear.

But I will out amid the sleet, and view
Each shrivelling stalk and silent-falling leaf.
Truth after truth, of choicest scent and hue,
Fades, and in fading stirs the Angels' grief,
Unanswer'd here; for she, once pattern chief
Of faith, my Country, now gross hearted grown,
Waits but to burn the stem before her idol's throne.

At Sea. *June 23, 1833.*

CONSOLATION

It is I; be not afraid.

WHEN I sink down in gloom or fear,
Hope blighted or delay'd,
Thy whisper, Lord, my heart shall cheer,
"'Tis I; be not afraid!"

Or, startled at some sudden blow,
If fretful thoughts I feel,
"Fear not, it is but I!" shall flow,
As balm my wound to heal.

Nor will I quit Thy way, though foes
Some onward pass defend;
From each rough voice the watchword goes,
"Be not afraid!...a friend!"

And oh! when judgment's trumpet clear
Awakes me from the grave,
Still in its echo may I hear,
"'Tis Christ; He comes to save."

At Sea. *June 23, 1833.*

UZZAH AND OBED-EDOM

THE ark of God has hidden strength;
Who reverence or profane,
They, or their seed, shall find at length
The penalty or gain.

While as a sojourner it sought
Of old its destined place,
A blessing on the home it brought
Of one who did it grace.

But there was one, outstripping all
The holy-vestured band,
Who laid on it, to save its fall,
A rude corrective hand.

Read, who the Church would cleanse, and mark
   How stern the warning runs;
There are two ways to aid her ark—
   As patrons, and as sons.

At Sea. *June 24, 1833.*

THE GIFT OF TONGUES.

ONCE cast with men of language strange
   And foreign-moulded creed,
I mark'd their random converse change,
   And sacred themes succeed.

Oh, how I coveted the gift
   To thread their mingled throng
Of sounds, then high my witness lift!
   But weakness chain'd my tongue.

Lord! has our dearth of faith and prayer
   Lost us this power once given,
Or is it sent at seasons rare
   And then flits back to heaven?

At Sea. *June 24, 1833.*

THE POWER OF PRAYER

THERE is not on the earth a soul so base
   But may obtain a place
   In convenanted grace;
So that his feeble prayer of faith obtains
   Some loosening of his chains,
And earnests of the great release, which rise
From gift to gift, and reach at length the eternal prize.

All may save self;—but minds that heavenward tower
   Aim at a wider power,
   Gifts on the world to shower.—
And this is not at once;—by fastings gain'd,
   And trials well sustain'd,
By pureness, righteous deeds, and toils of love,
Abidance in the Truth, and zeal for God above.

At Sea. *June 24, 1833.*

SEMITA JUSTORUM

WHEN I look back upon my former race,
Seasons I see at which the Inward Ray
More brightly burn'd, or guided some new way;
Truth, in its wealthier scene and nobler space
Given for my eye to range, and feet to trace.
And next I mark, 'twas trial did convey,
Or grief, or pain, or strange eventful day,
To my tormented soul such larger grace.
So now, whene'er, in journeying on, I feel
The shadow of the Providential Hand,
Deep breathless stirrings shoot across my breast,
Searching to know what He will now reveal,
What sin uncloak, what stricter rule command,
And girding me to work His full behest.

At Sea. *June 25, 1833.*

THE ELEMENTS

(A Tragic Chorus)

MAN is permitted much
To scan and learn
In Nature's frame;
Till he well-nigh can tame
Brute mischiefs and can touch
Invisible things, and turn
All warring ills to purposes of good.
Thus, as a god below,
He can control,
And harmonize, what seems amiss to flow
As sever'd from the whole
And dimly understood.

But o'er the elements
One Hand alone
One Hand has sway.
What influence day by day
In straiter belt prevents
The impious Ocean, thrown

Alternate o'er the ever-sounding shore?
  Or who has eye to trace
  How the Plague came?
Forerun the doublings of the Tempest's race?
Or the Air's weight and flame
On a set scale explore?

  Thus God has will'd
That man, when fully skill'd,
Still gropes in twilight dim;
Encompass'd all his hours
  By fearfullest powers
  Inflexible to him.
That so he may discern
  His feebleness,
And e'en for earth's success
  To Him in wisdom turn,
Who holds for us the keys of either home,
Earth and the world to come.

At Sea. *June 25, 1833.*

APOSTASY

FRANCE! I will think of thee as what thou wast,
  When Poictiers show'd her zeal for the true creed;
Or in that age, when Holy Truth, though cast
  On a rank soil, yet was a thriving seed,
Thy schools within, from neighbouring countries chased;
  E'en of thy pagan day I bear to read,
Thy Martyrs sanctified the guilty host,
The sons of blessèd John, rear'd on a western coast.

I dare not think of thee as what thou art,
  Lest thoughts too deep for man should trouble me.
It is not safe to place the mind and heart
  On brink of evil, or its flames to see,
Lest they should dizzy, or some taint impart,
  Or to our sin a fascination be.
And so in silence I will now proclaim
Hate of thy present self, and scarce will sound thy name[1].

Off the French Coast. *June 26, 1833.*

[1] This is not the language of one who knew any thing rightly of that great Catholic and highly gifted people.

JUDAISM

(A Tragic Chorus)

O PITEOUS race!
Fearful to look upon,
Once standing in high place,
Heaven's eldest son.
O aged blind
Unvenerable! as thou flittest by,
I liken thee to him in pagan song,
In thy gaunt majesty,
The vagrant King, of haughty-purposed mind
Whom prayer nor plague could bend[1];
Wrong'd, at the cost of him who did the wrong,
Accursed himself, but in his cursing strong,
And honour'd in his end.

O Abraham! sire,
Shamed in thy progeny;
Who to thy faith aspire,
Thy Hope deny.
Well wast thou given
From out the heathen an adopted heir,
Raised strangely from the dead when sin had slain
Thy former-cherish'd care.
O holy men, ye first-wrought gems of heaven!
Polluted in your kin,
Come to our fonts, your lustre to regain.
O Holiest Lord!...but Thou canst take no stain
Of blood, or taint of sin.

Twice in their day
Proffer of precious cost
Was made, Heaven's hand to stay
Ere all was lost.
The first prevail'd;
Moses was outcast from the promised home,
For his own sin, yet taken at his prayer
To change his people's doom.
Close on their eve, one other ask'd and fail'd;
When fervent Paul was fain
The accursèd tree, as Christ had borne, to bear,
No hopeful answer came,—a Price more rare
Already shed in vain.

Off Marseilles Harbour. *June 27, 1833.*

[1] Vide the Œdipus Coloneus of Sophocles.

SEPARATION OF FRIENDS

DO not their souls, who 'neath the Altar wait
    Until their second birth,
The gift of patience need, as separate
    From their first friends of earth?
Not that earth's blessings are not all outshone
    By Eden's Angel flame,
But that earth knows not yet, the Dead has won
    That crown, which was his aim.
For when he left it, 'twas a twilight scene
    About his silent bier,
A breathless struggle, faith and sight between,
    And Hope and sacred Fear.
Fear startled at his pains and dreary end,
    Hope raised her chalice high,
And the twin-sisters still his shade attend,
    View'd in the mourner's eye.
So day by day for him from earth ascends,
    As steam in summer-even,
The speechless intercession of his friends,
    Toward the azure heaven.
Ah! dearest, with a word he could dispel
    All questioning, and raise
Our hearts to rapture, whispering all was well,
    And turning prayer to praise.
And other secrets too he could declare,
    By patterns all divine,
His earthly creed retouching here and there,
    And deepening every line.
Dearest! he longs to speak, as I to know,
    And yet we both refrain:
It were not good: a little doubt below,
    And all will soon be plain[1].

Marseilles. *June 27, 1833.*

[1]The last twelve lines were added after Feb. 28, 1836, the date of R. Hurrell Froude's death.

MORNING

FROM ST. GREGORY NAZIANZEN

I RISE and raise my clasped hands to Thee!
Henceforth, the darkness hath no part in me,
Thy sacrifice this day;
Abiding firm, and with a freeman's might
Stemming the waves of passion in the fight;—
Ah, should I from Thee stray,
My hoary head, Thy table where I bow,
Will be my shame, which are mine honour now.
Thus I set out;—Lord! lead me on my way!

Oxford. *1834.*

EVENING

FROM ST. GREGORY NAZIANZEN

O HOLIEST Truth! how have I lied to Thee!
I vow'd this day Thy sacrifice to be;
But I am dim ere night.
Surely I made my prayer, and I did deem
That I could keep in me Thy morning beam,
Immaculate and bright.
But my foot slipp'd; and, as I lay, he came,
My gloomy foe, and robb'd me of heaven's flame,
Help Thou my darkness, Lord, till I am light.

Oxford. *1834.*

THE PRIESTLY OFFICE

FROM ST. GREGORY NAZIANZEN

IN service o'er the Mystic Feast I stand;
I cleanse Thy victim-flock, and bring them near
In holiest wise, and by a bloodless rite.
O Fire of Love! O gushing Fount of Light!
(As best I know, who need Thy cleansing Hand)
Dread office this, bemired souls to clear
Of their defilement, and again make bright.

Oxford. *1834.*

A HERMITAGE

FROM ST. GREGORY NAZIANZEN

SOME one whisper'd yesterday,
Of the rich and fashionable,
Gregory in his own small way
Easy was and comfortable.

Had he not of wealth his fill
Whom a garden gay did bless,
And a gently trickling rill,
And the sweets of idleness?

I made answer:—"Is it ease
Fasts to keep and tears to shed,
Vigil hours and wounded knees,
Call you these a pleasant bed?"

Thus a veritable monk
Does to death his fleshly frame;
Be there who in sloth are sunk,
They have forfeited the name.

Oxford. *1834.*

THE MARRIED AND THE SINGLE

A FRAGMENT FROM ST. GREGORY NAZIANZEN

AS, when the hand some mimic form would paint,
It marks its purpose first in shadows faint,
And next, its store of varied hues applies,
Till outlines fade, and the full limbs arise;
So in the earlier school of sacred lore
The Virgin-life no claim of honour bore,
While in Religion's youth the Law held sway,
And traced in symbols dim that better way.
But, when the Christ came by a Virgin-birth,—
His radiant passage from high heaven to earth,—
And, spurning father for His mortal state,
Did Eve and all her daughters consecrate,
Solved fleshly laws, and in the letter's place
Gave us the Spirit and the Word of Grace,

Then shone the glorious Celibate at length,
Robed in the dazzling lightnings of its strength.
Surpassing gifts of earth and marriage vow,
As soul the body, heaven this world below,
The eternal peace of saints life's troubled span,
And the high throne of God, the haunts of man.
So now there circles round the King of Light
A heaven on earth, a blameless court and bright,
Aiming as emblems of their God to shine,
Christ in their heart, and on their brow His Sign,—
Soft funeral lights in the world's twilight dim,
Loving their God, and ever loved by Him.

Ye countless multitudes, content to bow
To the soft thraldom of the marriage vow!
I mark your haughty step, your froward gaze,
Gems deck your hair, and silk your limbs arrays;
Come, tell the gain which wedlock has conferr'd
On man; and then the single shall be heard.

The married many thus might plead, I wean;
Right glib their tongue, full confident their mien:—
"Hear all who live! to whom the nuptial rite
Has brought the privilege of life and light.
We, who are wedded, but the law obey
Stamp'd at creation on our blood and clay,
What time the Demiurge our line began,
Oped Adam's side, and out of man drew man.
Thenceforth let children of a mortal sod
Honour the law of earth, the primal law of God.

"List, you shall hear the gifts of price that lie
Gather'd and bound within the marriage-tie.
What taught the arts of life, the truths which sleep
In earth, or highest heaven, or vasty deep?
What fill'd the mart, and urged the vessel brave
To link in one fair countries o'er the wave?
What raised the town? what gave the type and germ
Of social union, and of sceptre firm?
What the first husbandman, the glebe to plough,
And rear the garden, but the marriage vow?

"Nay, list again! Who seek its kindly chain,
A second self, a double presence gain;
Hands, eyes, and ears, to act or suffer here,
Till e'en the weak inspire both love and fear,—
A comrade's sigh, to soothe when cares annoy,
A comrade's smile, to elevate his joy.

"Nor say it weds us to a carnal life,
When want is urgent, fears and vows are rife.
Light heart is his, who has no yoke at home,
Scant prayer for blessings, as the seasons come;
But wife, and offspring, goods which go or stay,
Teach us our need, and life would be defaced,
A ghastly vision on a howling waste,
Stern, heartless, reft of the sweet spells which swage
The throes of passion, and which gladden age.
No child's sweet pranks, once more to make us young;
No ties of place about our heart-strings flung;
No public haunts to cheer; no festive tide
When harmless mirth and smiling wit preside;
A life which scorns the gifts by Heaven assign'd,
Nor knows the sympathy of human kind.

"Prophets and teachers, priests and victor kings,
Deck'd with each grace which heaven-taught nature brings,
These were no giant offspring of the earth,
But to the marriage-promise owed their birth:—
Moses and Samuel, David, David's Son,
The blessed Tishbite, the more blessed John,
The sacred Twelve in apostolic choir,
Strong-hearted Paul, instinct with seraph fire,
And others, now or erst, who to high heaven aspire.
Bethink ye; should the single state be best,
Yet who the single, but my offspring blest?
My sons, be still, nor with your parents strive:
They coupled in their day, and so ye live."

Thus marriage pleads. Now let her rival speak—
Dim is her downcast eye, and pale her cheek;
Untrimm'd her gear; no sandals on her feet;
A sparest form for austere tenant meet.

She drops her veil her modest face around,
And her lips open, but we hear no sound.
I will address her:—"Hail, O child of Heaven,
Glorious within! to whom a post is given
Hard by the Throne where angels bow and fear,
E'en while thou hast a name and mission here,
O deign thy voice, unveil thy brow, and see
Thy ready guard and minister in me.
Oft hast thou come heaven-wafted to my breast,
Bright Spirit! so come again, and give me rest."

..."Ah, who has hither drawn my backward feet,
Changing for wordly strife my lone retreat?
Where, in the silent chant of holy deeds,
I praise my God, and tend the sick soul's needs;
By toils of day, and vigils of the night,
By gushing tears, and blessed lustral rite.
I have no sway amid the crowd, no art
In speech, no plea in council or in mart.
Nor human law, nor judges throned on high,
Smile on my face, and to my words reply.
Let others seek earth's honours; be it mine
One law to cherish, and to track one line,
Straight on towards heaven to press with single bent,
To know and love my God, and then to die content."

Oxford. *1834.*

INTERCESSION OF THE SAINTS

WHILE Moses on the Mountain lay,
Night after night, and day by day,
Till forty suns were gone,
Unconscious, in the Presence bright,
Of lustrous day and starry night,
As though his soul had flitted quite
From earth, and Eden won;

The pageant of a kingdom vast,
And things unutterable, pass'd
  Before the Prophet's eye;
Dread shadows of th' Eternal Throne,
The fount of Life, and Altar-stone,
Pavement, and they that tread thereon,
  And those who worship nigh.

But lest he should his own forget,
Who in the vale were struggling yet,
  A sadder vision came,
Announcing all that guilty deed
Of idol rite, that in their need
He for his flock might intercede,
  And stay Heaven's rising flame.

Oxford. *September 4, 1835.*

WAITING FOR THE MORNING

Quoddam quasi pratum, in quo animæ nihil patiebantur, sed manebant, nondum idoneæ Visioni Beatæ. Bedæ Hist. v.

THEY are at rest:
  We may not stir the heaven of their repose
With loud-voiced grief, or passionate request,
    Or selfish plaint for those
Who in the mountain grots of Eden lie,
And hear the fourfold river, as it hurries by.

    They hear it sweep
In distance down the dark and savage vale;
But they at eddying pool or current deep,
    Shall never more grow pale;
They hear, and meekly muse, as fain to know
How long untired, unspent, that giant stream shall flow.

    And soothing sounds
Blend with the neighbouring waters as they glide;
Posted along the haunted garden's bounds
    Angelic forms abide,
Echoing, as words of watch, o'er lawn and grove,
The verses of that hymn which Seraphs chant above.

Oxford. *1835.*

MATINS—SUNDAY[1]

Primo die, quo Trinitas.

TO-DAY the Blessed Three in One
  Began the earth and skies;
To-day a Conqueror, God the Son,
  Did from the grave arise;
We too will wake, and, in despite
Of sloth and languor, all unite,
As Psalmists bid, through the dim night
  Waiting with wistful eyes.

So may He hear, and heed each vow
  And prayer to Him addrest;
And grant an instant cleansing now,
  A future glorious rest.
So may he plentifully shower,
On all who hymn His love and power,
In this most still and sacred hour,
  His sweetest gifts and best.

Father of purity and light!
  Thy presence if we win,
'Twill shield us from the deeds of night
  The burning darts of sin;
Lest aught defiled or dissolute
Relax our bodies or imbrute,
And fires eternal be the fruit
  Of fire now lit within.

Fix in our hearts, Redeemer dear,
  The ever-gushing spring
Of grace to cleanse, of life to cheer
  Souls sick and sorrowing.
Thee, bounteous Father, we intreat,
And only Son, awful and sweet,
And life-creating Paraclete,
  The everlasting King.

[1] This hymn and the following hymns are all free translations, made in 1836-38, from the Roman breviary, apart from two, which are from the Parisian.

MATINS—SUNDAY

Nocte surgentes.

LET us arise, and watch by night,
  And meditate always;
And chant, as in our Maker's sight,
  United hymns of praise.

So, singing with the Saints in bliss,
  With them we may attain
Life everlasting after this,
  And heaven for earthly pain.

Grant this, O Father, Only Son,
  And Spirit, God of grace,
To whom all worship shall be done
  In every time and place.

MATINS—MONDAY

Somno refectis artubus.

SLEEP has refresh'd our limbs, we spring
  From off our bed, and rise;
Lord, on Thy suppliants, while they sing,
  Look with a Father's eyes.

Be Thou the first on every tongue,
  The first in every heart;
That all our doings all day long,
  Holiest! from Thee may start.

Cleanse Thou the gloom, and bid the light
  Its healing beams renew;
The sins, which have crept in with night,
  With night shall vanish too.

Our bosoms, Lord, unburthen Thou,
  Let nothing there offend;
That those who hymn Thy praises now
  May hymn them to the end.

Grant this, O Father, Only Son,
And Spirit, God of grace,
To whom all worship shall be done
In every time and place.

MATINS—TUESDAY

Consors Paterni luminis.

O GOD from God, and Light from Light,
Who art Thyself the day,
Our chants shall break the clouds of night;
Be with us while we pray.

Chase Thou the gloom that haunts the mind,
The thronging shades of hell,
The sloth and drowsiness that bind
The senses with a spell.

Lord, to their sins indulgent be,
Who, in this hour forlorn,
By faith in what they do not see,
With songs prevent the morn.

Grant this, O Father, etc.

MATINS—WEDNESDAY

Rerum Creator optime.

WHO madest all and dost control,
Lord, with Thy touch divine,
Cast out the slumbers of the soul,
The rest that is not Thine.

Look down, Eternal Holiness,
And wash the sins away,
Of those, who, rising to confess,
Outstrip the lingering day.

Our hearts and hands by night, O Lord,
We lift them in our need;
As holy Psalmists give the word,
And holy Paul the deed.

Each sin to Thee of years gone by,
Each hidden stain lies bare;
We shrink not from Thine awful eye,
But pray that Thou wouldst spare.

Grant this, O Father, etc.

MATINS—THURSDAY

Nox atra rerum contegit.

ALL tender lights, all hues divine
The night has swept away;
Shine on us, Lord, and we shall shine
Bright in an inward day.

The spots of guilt, sin's wages base,
Searcher of hearts, we own;
Wash us and robe us in Thy grace,
Who didst for sins atone.

The sluggard soul, that bears their mark,
Shrinks in its silent lair,
Or gropes amid its chambers dark
For Thee, who art not there.

Redeemer! send Thy piercing rays,
That we may bear to be
Set in the light of Thy pure gaze,
And yet rejoice in Thee.

Grant this, O Father, etc.

MATINS—FRIDAY

Tu Trinitatis Unitas.

MAY the dread Three in One, who sways
All with His sovereign might,
Accept us for this hymn of praise,
His watchers in the night.

For in the night, when all is still,
We spurn our bed and rise,
To find the balm for ghostly ill,
His bounteous hand supplies.

If e'er by night our envious foe
    With guilt our souls would stain,
May the deep streams of mercy flow,
    And make us white again;

That so with bodies braced and bright,
    And hearts awake within,
All fresh and keen may burn our light,
    Undimm'd, unsoil'd by sin.

Shine on Thine own, Redeemer sweet!
    Thy radiance increate
Through the long day shall keep our feet
    In their pure morning state.

Grant this, O Father, etc.

MATINS—SATURDAY

Summæ Parens clementiæ.

FATHER of mercies infinite,
    Ruling all things that be,
Who, shrouded in the depth and height,
    Art One, and yet art Three;

Accept our chants, accept our tears,
    A mingled stream we pour;
Such stream the laden bosom cheers,
    To taste Thy sweetness more.

Purge Thou with fire the o'ercharged mind,
    Its sores and wounds profound;
And with the watcher's girdle bind
    The limbs which sloth has bound.

That they who with their chants by night
    Before Thy presence come,
All may be fill'd with strength and light
    From their eternal home.

Grant this, O Father, etc.

LAUDS—SUNDAY.

Æterne rerum conditor.

FRAMER of the earth and sky,
  Ruler of the day and night,
With a glad variety,
  Tempering all, and making light;

Gleams upon our dark path flinging,
  Cutting short each night begun,
Hark! for chanticleer is singing,
  Hark! he chides the lingering sun.

And the morning star replies,
  And lets loose the imprison'd day;
And the godless bandit flies
  From his haunt and from his prey.

Shrill it sounds, the storm relenting
  Soothes the weary seaman's ears;
Once it wrought a great repenting,
  In that flood of Peter's tears.

Rouse we; let the blithesome cry
  Of that bird our hearts awaken;
Chide the slumberers as they lie,
  And arrest the sin-o'ertaken.

Hope and health are in his strain,
  To the fearful and the ailing;
Murder sheathes his blade profane,
  Faith revives when faith was failing.,

Jesu, Master! when we sin,
  Turn on us Thy healing face;
It will melt the offence within
  Into penitential grace:

Beam on our bewilder'd mind,
  Till its dreamy shadows flee;
Stones cry out where Thou hast shined,
  Jesu! musical with Thee.

To the Father and the Son,
And the Spirit, who in Heaven
Ever witness, Three and One,
Praise in Earth be ever given.

LAUDS—SUNDAY

Ecce jam noctis.

PALER have grown the shades of night,
And nearer draws the day,
Checkering the sky with streaks of light,
Since we began to pray:

To pray for mercy when we sin,
For cleansing and release,
For ghostly safety, and within
For everlasting peace.

Praise to the Father, as is meet,
Praise to the Only Son,
Praise to the Holy Paraclete,
While endless ages run.

LAUDS—MONDAY

Splendor Paternæ gloriæ.

OF the Father Effluence bright,
Out of Light evolving light,
Light from Light, unfailing Ray,
Day creative of the day:

Truest Sun, upon us stream
With Thy calm perpetual beam,
In the Spirit's still sunshine
Making sense and thought divine.

Seek we too the Father's face,
Father of almighty grace,
And of majesty excelling,
Who can purge our tainted dwelling;

Who can aid us, who can break
Teeth of envious foes, and make
Hours of loss and pain succeed,
Guiding safe each duteous deed,

And infusing self-control,
Fragrant chastity of soul,
Faith's keen flame to soar on high,
Incorrupt simplicity.

Christ Himself for food be given,
Faith become the cup of Heaven,
Out of which the joy is quaff'd
Of the Spirit's sobering draught.

With that joy replenishèd,
Morn shall glow with modest red,
Noon with beaming faith be bright,
Eve be soft without twilight.

It has dawn'd;—upon our way.
Father in Thy Word, this day,
In Thy Father Word Divine,
From Thy cloudy pillar shine.

To the Father, and the Son,
And the Spirit, Three and One,
As of old, and as in Heaven,
Now and here be glory given.

LAUDS—TUESDAY

Ales diei nuntius.

DAY'S herald bird
At length is heard,
Telling its morning torch is lit,
And small and still
Christ's accents thrill,
Within the heart rekindling it.

Away, He cries,
With languid eyes,
And sickly slumbers profitless!
I am at hand,
As watchers stand,
In awe, and truth, and holiness.

He will appear
The hearts to cheer
Of suppliants pale and abstinent;
Who cannot sleep
Because they weep
With holy grief and violent.

Keep us awake,
The fetters break,
Jesu! which night has forged for us;
Yea, melt the night
To sinless light,
Till all is bright and glorious.

To Father, Son,
And Spirit, One,
To the Most Holy Trinity,
All praise be given
In Earth and Heaven,
Now, as of old, and endlessly.

LAUDS—WEDNESDAY

Nox et tenebræ et nubila.

HAUNTING gloom and flitting shades,
  Ghastly shapes, away!
Christ is rising, and pervades
  Highest Heaven with day.

He with His bright spear the night
  Dazzles and pursues;
Earth wakes up, and glows with light
  Of a thousand hues.

Thee, O Christ, and Thee alone,
  With a single mind,
We with chant and plaint would own;
  To Thy flock be kind.

Much it needs Thy light divine,
  Spot and stain to clean;
Light of Angels, on us shine
  With Thy face serene.

To the Father, and the Son,
  And the Holy Ghost,
Here be glory, as is done
  By the angelic host.

LAUDS—THURSDAY

Lux ecce surgit aurea.

SEE, the golden dawn is glowing,
While the paly shades are going,
Which have led us far and long,
In a labyrinth of wrong.

May it bring us peace serene;
May it cleanse, as it is clean;
Plain and clear our words be spoke,
And our thoughts without a cloak;

So the day's account, shall stand,
Guileless tongue and holy hand,
Stedfast eyes and unbeguiled,
"Flesh as of a little child."

There is One who from above
Watches how the still hours move
Of our day of service done,
From the dawn to setting sun.

To the Father, and the Son,
And the Spirit, Three and One,
As of old, and as in Heaven,
Now and here be glory given.

LAUDS—FRIDAY

Æterna coeli gloria.

GLORY of the eternal Heaven,
Blessed Hope to mortals given,
Of the Almighty Only Son,
And the Virgin's Holy One;
Raise us, Lord, and we shall rise
In a sober mood,
And a zeal, which glorifies
Thee from gratitude.

Now the day-star, keenly glancing,
Tells us of the Sun's advancing;
While the unhealthy shades decline,
Rise within us, Light Divine!
Rise, and, risen, go not hence,
Stay and make us bright,
Streaming through each cleansèd sense,
On the outward night.

Then the root of faith shall spread
In the heart new fashionèd;
Gladsome hope shall spring above,
And shall bear the fruit of love.
To the Father, and the Son,
And the Holy Ghost,
Here be glory, as is done
By the angelic host.

LAUDS—SATURDAY

Aurora jam spargit polum.

THE dawn is sprinkled o'er the sky.
The day steals softly on;
Its darts are scatter'd far and nigh,
And all that fraudful is, shall fly
Before the brightening sun;
Spectres of ill, that stalk at will,
And forms of guilt that fright,
And hideous sin, that ventures in
Under the cloak of night.

And of our crimes the tale complete,
Which bows us in Thy sight,
Up to the latest, they shall fleet,
Out-told by our full numbers sweet,
And melted by the light.
To Father, Son, and Spirit, One,
Whom we adore and love,
Be given all praise, now and always,
Here as in Heaven above.

PRIME

(FROM THE PARISIAN BREVIARY[1])

Jam lucis orto sidere.

NOW that the day-star glimmers bright,
We suppliantly pray
That He, the uncreated Light,
May guide us on our way.

No sinful word, nor deed of wrong,
Nor thoughts that idly rove;
But simple truth be on our tongue,
And in our hearts be love.

And, while the hours in order flow,
O Christ, securely fence
Our gates, beleaguer'd by the foe,—
The gate of ever sense.

And grant that to Thine honour, Lord,
  Our daily toil may tend;
That we begin it at Thy word,
  And in Thy favour end.

And, lest the flesh in its excess
  Should lord it o'er the soul,
Let taming abstinence repress
  The rebel, and control.

To God the Father glory be,
  And to His Only Son,
And to the Spirit, One and Three,
  While endless ages run.

Littlemore. *February, 1842.*

[1]Vide the Anglo-Norman History of Sir Francis Palgrave (Vol. iii. p. 588), who did the Author the honour of asking him for a translation of this hymn, as also of the Christe Pastorum later.

TERCE

Nunc Sancte nobis Spiritus.

COME, Holy Ghost, who ever One
Reignest with Father and with Son,
It is the hour, our souls possess
With Thy full flood of holiness.

Let flesh, and heart, and lips, and mind,
Sound forth our witness to mankind;
And love light up our mortal frame,
Till others catch the living flame.

Now to the Father, to the Son,
And to the Spirit, Three in One,
Be praise and thanks and glory given
By men on earth, by Saints in heaven.

SEXT

Rector potens, verax Deus.

O GOD, who canst not change nor fail,
Guiding the hours, as they roll by,
Bright'ning with beams the morning pale.
And burning in the mid-day sky,

Quench Thou the fires of hate and strife,
The wasting fever of the heart;
From perils guard our feeble life,
And to our souls Thy peace impart.

Grant this, O Father, Only Son,
And Holy Spirit, God of grace,
To whom all glory, Three in One,
Be given in every time and place.

NONE

Rerum Deus tenax vigor.

O GOD, unchangeable and true,
Of all the Life and Power,
Dispensing light in silence through
Every successive hour,

Lord, brighten our declining day,
That it may never wane,
Till death, when all things round decay
Brings back the morn again.

This grace on Thy redeem'd confer,
Father, Co-equal Son,
And Holy Ghost, the Comforter,
Eternal Three in One.

VESPERS—SUNDAY.

Lucis Creator optime.

FATHER of Lights, by whom each day
Is kindled out of night,
Who, when the heavens were made, didst lay
Their rudiments in light;

Thou, who didst bind and blend in one
  The glistening morn and evening pale,
Hear Thou our plaint, when light is gone,
  And lawlessness and strife prevail.

Hear, lest the whelming weight of crime
  Wreck us with life in view;
Lest thoughts and schemes of sense and time
  Earn us a sinner's due.

So may we knock at Heaven's door,
  And strive the immortal prize to win,
Continually and evermore
  Guarded without and pure within.

Grant this, O Father, Only Son,
  And Spirit, God of grace,
To whom all worship shall be done
  In every time and place.

VESPERS—MONDAY

Immense coeli conditor.

LORD of unbounded space,
  Who, lest the sky and main
Should mix, and heaven should lose its place,
  Didst the rude waters chain;

Parting the moist and rare,
  That rills on earth might flow
To soothe the angry flame, whene'er
  It ravens from below;

Pour on us of Thy grace
  The everlasting spring;
Lest our frail steps renew the trace
  Of the ancient wandering.

May faith in lustre grow,
And rear her star in heaven,
Paling all sparks of earth below,
Unquench'd by damps of even.

Grant it, O Father, Son,
And Holy Spirit of grace,
To whom be glory, Three in One,
In every time and place.

VESPERS—TUESDAY

Telluris alme conditor.

ALL-BOUNTIFUL Creator, who,
When Thou didst mould the world, didst drain
The waters from the mass, that so
Earth might immovable remain;

That its dull clods it might transmute
To golden flowers in vale or wood,
To juice of thirst-allaying fruit,
And grateful herbage spread for food;

Wash Thou our smarting wounds and hot,
In the cool freshness of Thy grace;
Till tears start forth the past to blot,
And cleanse and calm Thy holy place;

Till we obey Thy full behest,
Shun the world's tainted touch and breath,
Joy in what highest is and best,
And gain a spell to baffle death.

Grant it, O Father, Only Son,
And Holy Spirit, God of grace,
To whom all glory, Three in One,
Be given in every time and place.

VESPERS—WEDNESDAY

Coeli Deus sanctissime.

O LORD, who, thron'd in the holy height,
Through plains of ether didst diffuse
The dazzling beams of light,
In soft transparent hues;

Who didst, on the fourth day, in heaven
Light the fierce cresset of the sun,
And the meek moon at even,
And stars that wildly run;

That they might mark and arbitrate
'Twixt alternating night and day,
And tend the train sedate
Of months upon their way;

Clear, Lord, the brooding night within,
And clean these hearts for Thy abode,
Unlock the spell of sin,
Crumble its giant load.

Grant it, O Father, Only Son,
And Holy Spirit, God of Grace,
To whom all praise be done
In every time and place.

VESPERS—THURSDAY

Magnæ Deus potentiæ.

O GOD, who hast given
the sea and the sky,
To fish and to bird
for a dwelling to keep,
Both sons of the waters,
one low and one high,
Ambitious of heaven,
or sunk in the deep;

Save, Lord, Thy servants,
whom Thou hast new made
In a laver of blood,
lest they trespass and die;
Lest pride should elate,
or sin should degrade,
And they stumble on earth,
or be dizzied on high.

To the Father and Son
And the Spirit be done,
Now and always,
Glory and praise.

VESPERS—FRIDAY

Hominis superne Conditor.

WHOM all obey,—
Maker of man! who from Thy height
Badest the dull earth bring to light
All creeping things, and the fierce might
Of beasts of prey;—

And the huge make
Of wild or gentler animal,
Springing from nothing at Thy call,
To serve in their due time, and all
For sinners' sake;

Shield us from ill!
Come it by passion's sudden stress,
Lurk in our mind's habitual dress,
Or through our actions seek to press
Upon our will.

Vouchsafe the prize
Of sacred joy's perpetual mood,
And service-seeking gratitude,
And love to quell each strife or feud,
If it arise.

Grant it, O Lord!
To whom, the Father, only Son,
And Holy Spirit, Three in One,
In heaven and earth all praise be done,
With one accord.

VESPERS—SATURDAY

Jam sol recedit igneus.

THE red sun is gone,
Thou Light of the heart,
Blessed Three, Holy One,
To Thy servants a sun
Everlasting impart.

There were Lauds in the morn,
    Here are Vespers at even;
Oh, may we adorn
Thy Temple new born
    With our voices in Heaven.

To the Father be praise,
    And praise to the Son
And the Spirit always,
While the infinite days
    Of eternity run.

COMPLINE

Te lucis ante terminum.

NOW that the day-light dies away,
    By all Thy grace and love,
Thee, Maker of the World, we pray
    To watch our bed above.

Let dreams depart and phantoms fly,
    The offspring of the night,
Keep us, like shrines, beneath Thine eye,
    Pure in our foe's despite.

This grace on Thy redeem'd confer,
    Father, Co-equal Son,
And Holy Ghost, the Comforter,
    Eternal Three in One.

ADVENT—VESPERS

Creator alme siderum.

CREATOR of the starry pole,
    Saviour of all who live,
And light of every faithful soul,
    Jesu, these prayers receive.

Who, sooner than our foe malign
    Should triumph, from above
Didst come, to be the medicine
    Of a sick world, in love;

And the deep wounds to cleanse and cure
  Of a whole race, didst go,
Pure Victim, from a Virgin pure,
  The bitter Cross unto.

Who hast a Name, and hast a Power,
  The height and depth to sway,
And Angels bow, and devils cower,
  In transport or dismay;

Thou too shalt be our Judge at length;
  Lord, in Thy grace bestow
Thy weapons of celestial strength,
  And snatch us from the foe.

Honour and glory, power and praise,
  To Father, and to Son,
And Holy Ghost, be paid always,
  The Eternal Three in One.

ADVENT—MATINS

Verbum supernum prodiens.

SUPERNAL Word, proceeding from
  The Eternal Father's breast,
And in the end of ages come,
  To aid a world distrest;

Enlighten, Lord, and set on fire
  Our spirits with Thy love,
That, dead to earth, they may aspire
  And live to joys above.

That, when the judgment-seat on high
  Shall fix the sinner's doom,
And to the just a glad voice cry,
  Come to your destined home;

Safe from the black and yawning lake
  Of restless, endless pain,
We may the face of God partake,
  The bliss of heaven attain.

To God the Father, God the Son,
  And Holy Ghost, to Thee,
As heretofore, when time is done,
  Unending glory be.

ADVENT—LAUDS

En clara vox redarguit.

HARK, a joyful voice is thrilling,
  And each dim and winding way
Of the ancient Temple filling;
  Dreams, depart! for it is day.

Christ is coming!—from thy bed
  Earth-bound soul, awake and spring,—
With the sun new-risen to shed
  Health on human suffering.

Lo! to grant a pardon free,
  Comes a willing Lamb from Heaven;
Sad and tearful, hasten we,
  One and all, to be forgiven.

Once again He comes in light,
  Girding earth with fear and woe;
Lord! be Thou our loving Might,
  From our guilt and ghostly foe.

To the Father, and the Son,
  And the Spirit, who in Heaven
Ever witness, Three and One,
  Praise on earth be ever given.

THE TRANSFIGURATION—MATINS

Quicunque Christum quæritis.

O YE who seek the Lord,
  Lift up your eyes on high,
For there He doth the Sign accord
  Of his bright majesty.

We see a dazzling sight
  That shall outlive all time,
Older than depth or starry height,
  Limitless and sublime.

'Tis He for Isræl's fold
  And heathen tribes decreed,
The King to Abraham pledged of old
  And his unfailing seed.

Prophets foretold His birth,
  And witness'd when He came,
The Father speaks to all the earth
  To hear, and own His name.

To Jesus, who displays
  To babes His beaming face,
Be, with the Father, endless praise,
  And with the Spirit of grace. *Amen.*

THE TRANSFIGURATION—LAUDS.

Lux alma Jesu.

LIGHT of the anxious heart,
  Jesu, Thou dost appear,
To bid the gloom of guilt depart,
  And shed Thy sweetness here.

Joyous is he, with whom,
  God's Word, Thou dost abide;
Sweet Light of our eternal home,
  To fleshly sense denied.

Brightness of God above!
  Unfathomable grace!
Thy Presence be a fount of love
  Within Thy chosen place.

To Thee, whom children see,
  The Father ever blest,
The Holy Spirit, One and Three,
  Be endless praise addrest. *Amen.*

FOR A MARTYR

Deus tuorum militum.

O GOD, of Thy soldiers
the Portion and Crown,
Spare Thy people, who hymn
the praise of the Blest;
Earth's bitter joys,
its lures and its frown,
He scann'd them and scorn'd,
and so is at rest.

Thy Martyr he ran
all valiantly o'er
A highway of blood
for the prize Thou hast given.
We kneel at Thy feet,
and meekly implore,
That our pardon may wait
on his triumph in heaven.

Honour and praise
To the Father and Son
And the Spirit be done
Now and always. *Amen.*

FOR A CONFESSOR BISHOP

Christe Pastorum[1].

O THOU, of shepherds Prince and Head,
Now on a Bishop's festal-day
Thy flock to many a shrine have sped
Their vows to pay.

He to the high and dreadful throne
Urged by no false inspirings, prest,
Nor on hot daring of his own,
But Thy behest.

And so, that soldier good and tried,
From the full horn of heavenly grace,
Thy Spirit did anoint, to guide
Thy ransom'd race.

And he becomes a father true,
  Spending and spent, when troubles fall,
A pattern and a servant too,
    All things to all.

His pleading sets the sinner free,
  He soothes the sick, he lifts the low,
Powerful in word, deep teacher, he,
    To quell the foe.

Grant us, O Christ, his prayers above,
  And grace below to sing Thy praise,
The Father's power, the Spirit's love,
    Now and always.

Littlemore. *February 7, 1842.*

[1] From the Parisian Breviary.

ETHELWALD

(From St. Bede's Metrical History of St. Cuthbert.)

BETWEEN two comrades dear,
  Zealous and true as they,
Thou, prudent Ethelwald, didst bear
  In that high home the sway.

A man, who ne'er 'tis said,
  Would of his graces tell,
Or with what arms be triumphed
  Over the Dragon fell.

So down to us hath come
  A memorable word,
Which in unguarded season from
  His blessed lips was heard.

It chanced, that, as the Saint
  Drank in with faithful ear
Of Angel tones the whispers faint,
  Thus spoke a brother dear:

"Oh, why so many a pause,
  Thwarting thy words' full stream,
Till her dark line Oblivion draws
  Across the broken theme?"

He answered: "Till thou seal
  To sounds of earth thine ear,
Sweet friend, be sure thou ne'er shalt feel
  Angelic voices near."

But then the hermit blest
  A sudden change came o'er;
He shudders, sobs, and smites his breast,
  Is mute, then speaks once more:

"Oh, by the Name Most High,
  What I have now let fall,
Hush, till I lay me down to die,
  And go the way of all!"

Thus did a Saint in fear
  His gifts celestial hide;
Thus did an Angel standing near
  Proclaim them far and wide.

Littlemore. *1844.*

CANDLEMAS

(A Song.)

THE Angel-lights of Christmas morn,
  Which shot across the sky,
Away they pass at Candlemas,
  They sparkle and they die.

Comfort of earth is brief at best,
  Although it be divine;
Like funeral lights for Christmas gone,
  Old Simeon's tapers shine.

And then for eight long weeks and more
  We wait in twilight grey,
Till the high candle sheds a beam
  On Holy Saturday.

We wait along the penance-tide
   Of solemn fast and prayer;
While song is hush'd, and lights grow dim
   In the sin-laden air.

And while the sword in Mary's soul
   Is driven home, we hide
In our own hearts, and count the wounds
   Of passion and of pride.

And still, though Candlemas be spent
   And Alleluias o'er,
Mary is music in our need,
   And Jesus light in store.

The Oratory 1849.

THE PILGRIM QUEEN

(A Song.)

THERE sat a Lady
all on the ground,
Rays of the morning
circled her round,
Save thee, and hail to thee
Gracious and Fair,
In the chill twilight
what wouldst thou there?

"Here I sit desolate,"
sweetly said she,
"Though I'm a queen,
and my name is Marie:
Robbers have rifled
my garden and store,
Foes they have stolen
my heir from my bower.

"They said they could keep Him
far better than I,
In a palace all His,
planted deep and raised high.
'Twas a palace of ice,
hard and cold as were they,
And when summer came,
it all melted away.

"Next would they barter Him,
Him the Supreme,
For the spice of the desert,
and gold of the stream;
And me they bid wander
in weeds and alone,
In this green merry land
which once was my own."

I look'd on that Lady,
        and out from her eyes
Came the deep glowing blue
        of Italy's skies;
And she raised up her head
        and she smiled, as a Queen
On the day of her crowning,
        so bland and serene.

"A moment," she said,
        "and the dead shall revive;
The giants are failing,
        the Saints are alive;
I am coming to rescue
        my home and my reign,
And Peter and Philip
        are close in my train."

The Oratory. 1849.

THE MONTH OF MARY

(A Song.)

GREEN are the leaves, and sweet the flowers,
  And rich the hues of May;
We see them in the gardens round,
  And market-panniers gay:
And e'en among our streets, and lanes,
  And alleys, we descry,
By fitful gleams, the fair sunshine,
  The blue transparent sky.

CHORUS

O Mother maid, be thou our aid,
  Now in the opening year;
Lest sights of earth to sin give birth,
  And bring the tempter near.

Green is the grass, but wait awhile,
'Twill grow, and then will wither;
The flowrets, brightly as they smile,
Shall perish altogether:
The merry sun, you sure would say,
It ne'er could set in gloom;
But earth's best joys have all an end,
And sin, a heavy doom.

CHORUS

But Mother maid, thou dost not fade;
With stars above thy brow,
And the pale moon beneath thy feet,
For ever throned art thou.

The green green grass, the glittering grove,
The heaven's majestic dome,
They image forth a tenderer bower,
A more refulgent home;
They tell us of that Paradise
Of everlasting rest,
And that high Tree, all flowers and fruit,
The sweetest, yet the best.

CHORUS

O Mary, pure and beautiful,
Thou art the Queen of May;
Our garlands wear about thy hair,
And they will ne'er decay.

The Oratory. *1850.*

THE QUEEN OF SEASONS

(A Song for an inclement May.)

ALL is divine
which the Highest has made,
Through the days that he wrought,
till the day when He stay'd;
Above and below,
within and around,
From the centre of space,
to its uttermost bound.

In beauty surpassing
the Universe smiled,
On the morn of its birth,
like an innocent child,
Or like the rich bloom,
of some delicate flower
And the Father rejoiced
in the work of His power.

Yet worlds brighter still,
and a brighter than those,
And a brighter again,
He had made, had he chose;
And you never could name
that conceivable best,
To exhaust the resources
the Maker possess'd.

But I know of one work
of His Infinite Hand,
Which special and singular
ever must stand;
So perfect, so pure,
and of gifts such a store,
That even Omnipotence
ne'er shall do more.

The freshness of May,
and the sweetness of June,
And the fire of July
in its passionate noon,
Munificent August,
September serene,
Are together no match
for my glorious Queen.

O Mary, all months
and all days are thine own,
In thee lasts their joyousness,
when they are gone;
And we give to thee May,
not because it is best,
But because it comes first,
and is pledge of the rest.

The Oratory. *1850.*

VALENTINE TO A LITTLE GIRL

LITTLE Maiden, dost thou pine
  For a faithful Valentine?
Art thou scanning timidly
Every face that meets thine eye?
Art thou fancying there may be
Fairer face than thou dost see?
Little maiden, scholar mine,
Wouldst thou have a Valentine?

Go and ask, my little child,
Ask the Mother undefiled:
Ask, for she will draw thee near,
And will whisper in thine ear:—
"Valentine! the name is good;
  For it comes of lineage high,
  And a famous family:
And it tells of gentle blood,
Noble blood,—and nobler still,
  For its owner freely pour'd
Every drop there was to spill
  In the quarrel of his Lord.
Valentine! I know the name,
Many martyrs bear the same;
And they stand in glittering ring
Round their warrior God and King,—
  Who before and for them bled,—
  With their robes of ruby red,
And their swords of cherub flame."

Yes! there is a plenty there,
Knights without reproach or fear,—
Such St. Denys, such St. George,
  Martin, Maurice, Theodore,
  And a hundred thousand more;
  Guerdon gain'd and warfare o'er,
By that sea without a surge,

And beneath the eternal sky,
 And the beatific Sun,
  In Jerusalem above,
 Valentine is every one;
Choose from out that company
  Whom to serve, and whom to love.

The Oratory. *1850.*

ST. PHILIP NERI IN HIS MISSION

(A Song.)

IN the far North our lot is cast,
 Where faithful hearts are few;
Still are we Philip's children dear,
 And Peter's soldiers true.

Founder and Sire! to mighty Rome,
 Beneath St. Peter's shade,
Early thy vow of loyal love
 And ministry was paid.

The solemn porch, and portal high,
 Of Peter was thy home;
The world's Apostle he, and thou
 Apostle of his Rome.

And first in the old catacombs,
 In galleries long and deep,
Where martyr Popes had ruled the flock,
 And slept their glorious sleep,

There didst thou pass the nights in prayer,
 Until at length there came,
Down on thy breast, new lit for thee,
 The Pentecostal flame;—

Then, in that heart-consuming love,
 Didst walk the city wide,
And lure the noble and the young
 From Babel's pomp and pride;

And, gathering them within thy cell,
 Unveil the lustre bright,
And beauty of thy inner soul,
 And gain them by the sight.

And thus to Rome, for Peter's faith
 Far known, thou didst impart
Thy lessons of the hidden life,
 And discipline of heart.

And as the Apostle, on the hill,
 Facing the Imperial Town,
First gazed upon his fair domain,
 Then on the cross lay down,

So thou, from out the streets of Rome
 Didst turn thy failing eye
Unto that mount of martyrdom[1],
 Take leave of it, and die.

The Oratory. *1850.*

[1] On the day of his death, Philip, "at the beginning of his Mass, remained for some time looking fixedly at the hill of St. Onofrio, which was visible from the chapel, just as if he saw some great vision. On coming to the Gloria in Excelsis, he began to sing, which was a very unusual thing for him, and he sang the whole of it with the greatest joy and devotion," &c.—Bacci's Life.

ST. PHILIP IN HIMSELF

(A Song.)

THE holy Monks, conceal'd from men,
 In midnight choir, or studious cell,
In sultry field, or wintry glen,
 The holy Monks, I love them well,

The Friars too, the zealous band
 By Dominic or Francis led,
They gather, and they take their stand
 Where foes are fierce, or friends have fled.

And then the unwearied Company,
 Which bears the Name of sacred might,
The Knights of Jesus, they defy
 The fiend,—full eager for the fight.

Yet there is one I more affect
    Than Jesuit, Hermit, Monk, or Friar,
'Tis an old man of sweet aspect,
    I love him more, I more admire.

I know him by his head of snow,
    His ready smile, his keen full eye,
His words which kindle as they flow,
    Save he be rapt in ecstasy.

He lifts his hands, there issues forth
    A fragrance virginal and rare,
And now he ventures to our North,
    Where hearts are frozen as the air.

He comes, by grace of his address,
    By the sweet music of his face,
And his low tones of tenderness,
    To melt a noble, stubborn race.

O sainted Philip, Father dear,
    Look on thy little ones, that we
Thy loveliness may copy here,
    And in the eternal Kingdom see.

The Oratory. *1850.*

ST. PHILIP IN HIS GOD

PHILIP, on thee the glowing ray
    Of heaven came down upon thy prayer,
To melt thy heart, and burn away
    All that of earthly dross was there.

Thy soul became as purest glass,
    Through which the Brightness Increate
In undimm'd majesty might pass,
    Transparent and illuminate.

And so, on Philip when we gaze,
    We see the image of his Lord;
The Saint dissolves amid the blaze
    Which circles round the Living Word.

The Meek, the Wise, none else is here,
  Dispensing light to men below;
His awful accents fill the ear,
  Now keen as fire, now soft as snow.

As snow, those inward pleadings fall,
  As soft, as bright, as pure, as cool,
With gentle weight and gradual,
  And sink into the feverish soul.

The Sinless One, He comes to seek,
  The dreary heart, the spirit lone,
Tender of natures proud or weak,
  Not less than if they were His own.

He takes and scans the sinner o'er,
  Handling His scholars one by one,
Weighing what they can bear, before
  He gives the penance to be done.

Jesu, to Philip's sons reveal
  That gentlest wisdom from above,
To spread compassion o'er their zeal,
  And mingle patience with their love.

The Oratory. *1850.*

GUARDIAN ANGEL

MY oldest friend, mine from the hour
  When first I drew my breath;
My faithful friend, that shall be mine,
  Unfailing, till my death;

Thou hast been ever at my side;
  My Maker to thy trust
Consign'd my soul, what time He framed
  The infant child of dust.

No beating heart in holy prayer,
  No faith, inform'd aright,
Gave me to Joseph's tutelage,
  Or Michæl's conquering might.

Nor patron Saint, nor Mary's love,
  The dearest and the best,
Has known my being, as thou hast known,
  And blest, as thou hast blest.

Thou wast my sponsor at the font;
  And thou, each budding year,
Didst whisper elements of truth
  Into my childish ear.

And when, ere boyhood yet was gone,
  My rebel spirit fell,
Ah! thou didst see, and shudder too,
  Yet bear each deed of Hell.

And then in turn, when judgments came,
  And scared me back again,
Thy quick soft breath was near to soothe
  And hallow every pain.

Oh! who of all thy toils and cares
  Can tell the tale complete,
To place me under Mary's smile,
  And Peter's royal feet!

And thou wilt hang about my bed,
  When life is ebbing low;
Of doubt, impatience, and of gloom,
  The jealous sleepless foe.

Mine, when I stand before the Judge;
  And mine, if spared to stay
Within the golden furnace, till
  My sin is burn'd away.

And mine, O Brother of my soul,
  When my release shall come;
Thy gentle arms shall lift me then,
  Thy wings shall waft me home.

The Oratory. *1853.*

THE GOLDEN PRISON

WEEP not for me, when I am gone,
 Nor spend thy faithful breath
In grieving o'er the spot or hour
 Of all-enshrouding death;

Nor waste in idle praise thy love
 On deeds of head or hand,
Which live within the living Book,
 Or else are writ in sand;

But let it be thy best of prayers,
 That I may find the grace
To reach the holy house of toll,
 The frontier penance-place,—

To reach that golden palace bright,
 Where souls elect abide,
Waiting their certain call to Heaven,
 With Angels at their side;

Where hate, nor pride, nor fear torments
 The transitory guest,
But in the willing agony
 He plunges, and is blest.

And as the fainting patriarch gain'd
 His needful halt mid-way,
And then refresh'd pursued his path,
 Where up the mount it lay,

So pray, that, rescued from the storm
 Of heaven's eternal ire,
I may lie down, then rise again,
 Safe, and yet saved by fire.

The Oratory. *1853.*

HEATHEN GREECE

(A Song.)

WHERE are the Islands of the Blest?
They stud the Ægean Sea;
And where the deep Elysian rest?
It haunts the vale where Peneus strong
Pours his incessant stream along,
While craggy ridge and mountain bare
Cut keenly through the liquid air,
And, in their own pure tints array'd,
Scorn earth's green robes which change and fade,
And stand in beauty undecay'd,
Guards of the bold and free.

For what is Afric, but the home
Of burning Phlegethon?
What the low beach and silent gloom,
And chilling mists of that dull river,
Along whose bank the thin ghosts shiver,—
The thin wan ghosts that once were men,—
But Tauris, isle of moor and fen,
Or, dimly traced by seamen's ken,
The pale-cliff'd Albion.

The Oratory. *1856.*

A MARTYR CONVERT

(A Hymn.)

THE number of Thine own complete,
Sum up and make an end;
Sift clean the chaff, and house the wheat;
And then, O Lord, descend.

Descend, and solve by that descent
This mystery of life;
Where good and ill, together blent,
Wage an undying strife.

For rivers twain are gushing still,
And pour a mingled flood;
Good in the very depths of ill,
Ill in the heart of good.

The last are first, the first are last,
  As angel eyes behold;
These from the sheep-cote sternly cast,
  Those welcomed to the fold.

No Christian home, no pastor's eye,
  No preacher's vocal zeal,
Moved Thy dear Martyr to defy
  The prison and the wheel.

Forth from the heathen ranks she stept,
  The forfeit crown to claim
Of Christian souls who had not kept
  Their birthright and their name.

Grace form'd her out of sinful dust;
  She knelt a soul defiled,
She rose in all the faith, and trust,
  And sweetness of a child.

And in the freshness of that love,
  She preach'd, by word and deed,
The mysteries of the world above,
  Her new-found, glorious creed.

And running, in a little hour,
  Of life the course complete.
She reach'd the Throne of endless power,
  And sits at Jesu's feet.

Her spirit there, her body here,
  Make one the earth and sky;
We use her name, we touch her bier,
  We know her God is nigh.

Praise to the Father, as is meet,
  Praise to the Only Son,
Praise to the Holy Paraclete
  While endless ages run.

The Oratory. *1856.*

ST. PHILIP IN HIS SCHOOL

(A Song.)

THIS is the Saint of gentleness and kindness,
 Cheerful in penance, and in precept winning;
Patiently healing of their pride and blindness,
 Souls that are sinning.

This is the Saint, who, when the world allures us,
 Cries her false wares, and opes her magic coffers,
Points to a better city, and secures us
 With richer offers.

Love is his bond, he knows no other fetter,
 Asks not our all, but takes whate'er we spare him,
Willing to draw us on from good to better,
 As we can bear him.

When he comes near to touch us and to bless us,
 Prayer is so sweet, that hours are but a minute;
Mirth is so pure, though freely it possess us,
 Sin is not in it.

Thus he conducts by holy paths and pleasant,
 Innocent souls, and sinful souls forgiven,
Towards the bright palace where our God is present,
 Throned in high heaven.

The Oratory. *1857.*

ST. PHILIP IN HIS DISCIPLES

(A Song.)

I ASK not for fortune, for silken attire,
For servants to throng me, and crowds to admire;
I ask not for power, or for name or success,
These do not content me, these never can bless.

Let the world flaunt her glories! each glittering prize,
Though tempting to others, is naught in my eyes.
A child of St. Philip, my master and guide,
I would live as he lived, and would die as he died.

Why should I be sadden'd, though friendless I be?
For who in his youth was so lonely as he?
If spited and mock'd, so was he, when he cried
To his God on the cross to stand by his side.

If scanty my fare, yet how was he fed?
On olives and herbs and a small roll of bread.
Are my joints and bones sore with aches and with pains?
Philip scourged his young flesh with fine iron chains.

A closet his home, where he, year after year,
Bore heat or cold greater than heat or cold here;
A rope stretch'd across it, and o'er it he spread
His small stock of clothes; and the floor was his bed.

One lodging besides; God's temple he chose,
And he slept in its porch his few hours of repose;
Or studied by light which the altar-lamp gave,
Or knelt at the Martyr's victorious grave.

I'm ashamed of myself, of my tears and my tongue,
So easily fretted, so often unstrung;
Mad at trifles, to which a chance moment gives birth;
Complaining of heaven, and complaining of earth.

So now, with his help, no cross will I fear,
But will linger resign'd through my pilgrimage here.
A child of St. Philip, my master and guide,
I will live as he lived, and will die as he died.

The Oratory. *1857.*

FOR THE DEAD

(A Hymn.)

HELP, Lord, the souls which Thou has made,
The souls to Thee so dear,
In prison, for the debt unpaid
Of sins committed here.

Those holy souls, they suffer on,
Resign'd in heart and will,
Until Thy high behest is done,
And justice has its fill.

For daily falls, for pardon'd crime,
  They joy to undergo
The shadow of Thy cross sublime,
  The remnant of Thy woe.

Help, Lord, the souls which Thou has made,
  The souls to Thee so dear,
In prison for the debt unpaid
  Of sins committed here.

Oh, by their patience of delay,
  Their hope amid their pain,
Their sacred zeal to burn away
  Disfigurement and stain;
Oh, by their fire of love, not less
  In keenness than the flame,
Oh, by their very helplessness,
  Oh, by Thy own great Name,

Good Jesu, help! sweet Jesu, aid
  The souls to Thee most dear,
In prison for the debt unpaid
  Of sins committed here.

The Oratory. 1857.

TO EDWARD CASWALL

(A gift for the New Year in return for his volume of Poems.)

ONCE, o'er a clear calm pool,
  The fulness of an over-brimming spring,
I saw the hawthorn and the chestnut fling
Their willing arms, of vernal blossoms full
And light green leaves: the lilac too was there,
The prodigal laburnum, dropping gold,
While the rich gorse along the turf crept near,
Close to the fountain's margin, and made bold
To peep into that pool, so calm and clear:—
As if well pleased to see their image bright
Reflected back upon their innocent sight;
Each flower and blossom shy
Lingering the live-long day in still delight,
Yet without touch of pride, to view,
Yea, with a tender, holy sympathy,
What was itself, yet was another too.

So on thy verse, my Brother and my Friend,
—The fresh upwelling of thy tranquil spirit,—
I see a many angel forms attend;
And gracious souls elect;
And thronging sacred shades, that shall inherit
One day the azure skies;
And peaceful saints, in whitest garments deck'd;
And happy infants of the second birth:—
These, and all other plants of paradise,
Thoughts from above, and visions that are sure,
And providences past, and memories dear,
In much content hang o'er that mirror pure,
And recognize each other's faces there,
And see a heaven on earth.

The Oratory. *January 1, 1858.*

THE TWO WORLDS

UNVEIL, O Lord, and on us shine
In glory and in grace;
This gaudy world grows pale before
The beauty of Thy face.

Till Thou art seen, it seems to be
A sort of fairy ground,
Where suns unsetting light the sky,
And flowers and fruits abound.

But when Thy keener, purer beam
Is pour'd upon our sight,
It loses all its power to charm,
And what was day is night,

Its noblest toils are then the scourge
Which made Thy blood to flow;
Its joys are but the treacherous thorns
Which circled round Thy brow.

And thus, when we renounce for Thee
Its restless aims and fears,
The tender memories of the past,
The hopes of coming years,

Poor is our sacrifice, whose eyes
Are lighted from above;
We offer what we cannot keep,
What we have ceased to love.

The Oratory. *1862.*

ST. MICHÆL

(A Hymn.)

THOU champion high
Of Heaven's imperial Bride,
For ever waiting on her eye,
Before her onward path, and at her side,
In war her guard secure, by night her ready guide!

To thee was given,
When those false angels rose
Against the Majesty of Heaven,
To hurl them down the steep, and on them close
The prison where they roam in hopeless unrepose.

Thee, Michæl, thee,
When sight and breathing fail,
The disembodied soul shall see;
The pardon'd soul with solemn joy shall hail,
When holiest rites are spent, and tears no more avail.

And thou, at last,
When Time itself must die,
Shalt sound that dread and piercing blast,
To wake the dead, and rend the vaulted sky,
And summon all to meet the Omniscient Judge on high.

The Oratory. *1862.*

MY BIRTHDAY

LET the sun summon all his beams to hold
   Bright pageant in his court, the cloud-paved sky;
Earth trim her fields and leaf her copses cold;
   Till the dull month with summer-splendours vie.
   It is my birthday;— and I fain would try,
Albeit in rude, in heartfelt strains to praise
   My God, for He hath shielded wondrously
From harm and envious error all my ways,
And purged my misty sight, and fixed on heaven my gaze.

Not in that mood, in which the insensate crowd
   Of wealthy folly hail their natal day,—
With riot throng, and feast, and greetings loud,
   Chasing away all thoughts of God and heaven away.
   Poor insect! feebly daring, madly gay,
What! joy because the fulness of the year
   Marks thee tor greedy death a riper prey?
Is not the silence of the grave too near?
Viewest thou the end with glee, meet scene for harrowing fear?

Go then infatuate! where the festive hall,
   The curious board, the oblivious wine invite;
Speed with obsequious haste at Pleasure's call,
   And with thy revels scare the far-spent night.
   Joy thee, that clearer dawn upon thy sight
The gates of death;— and pride thee in thy sum
   Of guilty years, and thy increasing white
Of locks; in age untimely frolicksome,
Make much of thy brief span, few years are yet to come!

Yet wiser such, than he whom blank despair
   And fostered grief's ungainful toil enslave;
Lodged in whose furrowed brow thrives fretful care,
   Sour graft of blighted hope; who, when the wave
   Of evil rushes, yields,— yet claims to rave
At his own deed, as the stern will of heaven.
   In sooth against his Maker idly brave,
Whom e'en the creature-world has tossed and driven,
Cursing the life he mars, "a boon so kindly given."[1]

He dreams of mischief; and that brainborn ill
Man's open face bears in his jealous view.
Fain would he fly to his doom; that doom is still
His own black thoughts, and they must aye pursue.
Too proud for merriment, or the pure dew
Soft glistening on the sympathising cheek;
As some dark, lonely evil-natured yew,
Whose poisonous fruit— so fabling poets speak—
Beneath the moon's pale gleam the midnight hag doth seek.

No! give to me, Great Lord, the constant soul,
Nor fooled by pleasure nor enslaved by care;
Each rebel-passion (for Thou canst) controul,
And make me know the tempter's every snare.
What, thou alone my sober hours I wear,
No friend in view, and sadness o'er my mind
Throws her dark veil?— Thou but accord this prayer
And I will bless thee for my birth, and find
That stillness breathes sweet tones, and solitude is kind.

Each coming year, O grant it to refine
All purer motions of this anxious breast:
Kindle the steadfast flame of love divine,
And comfort me with holier thoughts possest;
Till this worn body slowly sink to rest,
This feeble spirit to the sky aspire,—
As some long-prisoned dove towards her nest—
There to receive the gracious full-toned lyre,
Bowed low before the Throne 'mid the bright seraph choir.

Oxford *February 21, 1819*[2]

[1] "Is life a boon so kindly given," etc, vide Childe Harold, Canto ii.

[2] The diction of these Verses has been altered in some places at a later date.

SUPERSTITION

O LORD and Christ, Thy children of the South
So shudder, when they see
The two-edged sword sharp-issuing form Thy mouth,
As to fall back from Thee,
And cling to charms of man, or heathen rite
To aid them against Thee, Thou Fount of love and light!

But I before Thine awful eyes will go
And firmly fix me there,
In my full shame; not bent my doom to know,
Not fainting with despair;
Not fearing less than they, but deeming sure,
If e'en Thy Name shall fail, nought my base heart can cure.

Lazaret, Malta. *January 21 1833*

SYMPATHY

SOULS of the Just, I call not you
To share this joy with me,
This joy and wonder at the view
Of mountain, plain and sea;

Ye, on the loftier mountains old
Safe-lodged in Eden's cell,
Whence run the rivers four, behold
This earth, as ere it fell.

Or, when you think of those who stay
Still tried by the world's fight,
'Tis but in looking for the day
Which shall the loss unite.

Ye rather elder Spirits strong!
Who from the first have trod
This nether scene, man's race among,
The while you live to God,

Ye see, and ye can sympathise—
Vain thought! their mighty ken
Fills height and depth, the stars, the skies,
They smile at dim-eyed men.

Ah, Saviour! I perforce am Thine,
Angel and Saint apart:
Those searching Eyes are all-divine,
All-human is that Heart.

Agosta. *April 29, 1833.*

REVERENCE

I BOW at Jesu's name for 'tis the Sign
Of awful mercy towards a guilty line.
Of shameful ancestry, in birth defiled,
    And upwards from a child
Full of unlovely thoughts and rebel aims
    And scorn of judgment-flames,
How without fear can I behold my Life,
The Just assailing sin, and death-stain'd in the strife?

And so, albeit His woe in our release,
Thought of that woe aye dims our earthly peace;
The Life is hidden in a Fount of Blood!
    And this is tidings good
For souls, who, pierced that they have caused that woe
    Are fain to share it too;
But for the many, clinging to their lot
Of worldly ease and sloth, 'tis written "Touch Me not."

Off Monte Pellegrino. *June 14 1833*

SAMARIA

O RAIL not at our kindred in the North,
Albeit Samaria finds her likeness there;
A well-formed Priesthood, and the Church cast forth
    To the chill mountain air.

What, though their fathers sinned, and lost the grace
  Which seals the Holy Apostolic line?
Christ's love o'erflows the bounds His prophets trace
    In His reveal'd design.

Israel had seers; to them the word is nigh;
  Shall not that word run forth, and gladness give
To many a Shunammite, till in His eye
    The full Seven-thousand live?

Off Sardinia. *June 17,1833*

THE DREAM OF GERONTIUS

§1

GERONTIUS

JESU, MARIA—I am near to death,
And Thou art calling me; I know it now.
Not by the token of this faltering breath,
This chill at heart, this dampness on my brow,—
(Jesu, have mercy! Mary, pray for me!)
'Tis this new feeling, never felt before,
(Be with me, Lord, in my extremity!)
That I am going, that I am no more.
'Tis this strange innermost abandonment,
(Lover of souls! great God! I look to Thee,)
This emptying out of each constituent
And natural force, by which I come to be.
Pray for me, O my friends; a visitant
Is knocking his dire summons at my door,
The like of whom, to scare me and to daunt,
Has never, never come to me before;
'Tis death,—O loving friends, your prayers!—'tis he!...
As though my very being had given way,
As though I was no more a substance now,
And could fall back on nought to be my stay,
(Help, loving Lord! Thou my sole Refuge, Thou,)
And turn no whither, but must needs decay
And drop from out the universal frame
Into that shapeless, scopeless, blank abyss,
That utter nothingness, of which I came:
This is it that has come to pass in me;
Oh, horror! this it is, my dearest, this;
So pray for me, my friends, who have not strength to pray.

ASSISTANTS

Kyrie eleïson, Christe eleïson, Kyrie eleïson.
Holy Mary, pray for him.
All holy Angels, pray for him.
Choirs of the righteous, pray for him.
Holy Abraham, pray for him.
St. John Baptist, St. Joseph, pray for him.
St. Peter, St. Paul, St. Andrew, St. John,

All Apostles, all Evangelists, pray for him.
All holy Disciples of the Lord, pray for him.
All holy Innocents, pray for him.
All holy Martyrs, All holy Confessors,
All holy Hermits, all holy Virgins,
All ye Saints of God, pray for him.

GERONTIUS

Rouse thee, my fainting soul, and play the man;
  And through such waning span
Of life and thought as still has to be trod,
  Prepare to meet thy God.
And while the storm of that bewilderment
  Is for a season spent,
And, ere afresh the ruin on me fall,
  Use well the interval.

ASSISTANTS

Be merciful, be gracious; spare him, Lord.
Be merciful, be gracious; Lord, deliver him.
From the sins that are past;
  From Thy frown and Thine ire;
  From the perils of dying;
  From any complying
  With sin, or denying
  His God, or relying
On self, at the last;
  From the nethermost fire;
From all that is evil;
From power of the devil;
Thy servant deliver,
For once and for ever.

By Thy birth, and by Thy Cross,
Rescue him from endless loss;
By Thy death and burial,
Save him from a final fall;
By Thy rising from the tomb,
  By Thy mounting up above,
  By the Spirit's gracious love,
Save him in the day of doom.

GERONTIUS

Sanctus fortis, Sanctus Deus,
  De profundis oro te,
Miserere, Judex meus,
  Parce mihi, Domine.
Firmly I believe and truly
  God is Three, and God is One;
And I next acknowledge duly
  Manhood taken by the Son.
And I trust and hope most fully
  In that manhood crucified;
And each thought and deed unruly
  Do to death, as He has died.
Simply to His grace and wholly
  Light and life and strength belong,
And I love, supremely, solely,
  Him the holy, Him the strong.
Sanctus fortis, Sanctus Deus,
  De profundis oro te,
Miserere, Judex meus,
  Parce mihi, Domine.
And I hold in veneration,
  For the love of Him alone,
Holy Church, as His creation,
  And her teachings, as His own.
And I take with joy whatever
  Now besets me, pain or fear,
And with a strong will I sever
  All the ties which bind me here.
Adoration aye be given,
  With and through the angelic host,
To the God of earth and heaven,
  Father, Son, and Holy Ghost.
Sanctus fortis, Sanctus Deus,
  De profundis oro te,
Miserere, Judex meus,
  Mortis in discrimine.

I can no more; for now it comes again,
That sense of ruin, which is worse than pain,
That masterful negation and collapse
Of all that makes me man; as though I bent
Over the dizzy brink
Of some sheer infinite descent;
Or worse, as though
Down, down for ever I was falling through
The solid framework of created things,
And needs must sink and sink
Into the vast abyss. And, crueller still,
A fierce and restless fright begins to fill
The mansion of my soul. And, worse and worse,
Some bodily form of ill
Floats on the wind, with many a loathsome curse
Tainting the hallow'd air, and laughs, and flaps
Its hideous wings,
And makes me wild with horror and dismay.
O Jesu, help! pray for me, Mary, pray!
Some Angel, Jesu! such as came to Thee
In Thine own agony...
Mary, pray for me. Joseph, pray for me. Mary, pray for me.

ASSISTANTS

Rescue him, O Lord, in this his evil hour,
As of old so many by Thy gracious power:—
(Amen.)
Enoch and Elias from the common doom;
(Amen.)
Noe from the waters in a saving home;
(Amen.)
Abraham from th' abounding guilt of Heathenesse;
(Amen.)
Job from all his multiform and fell distress;
(Amen.)
Isaac, when his father's knife was raised to slay;
(Amen.)
Lot from burning Sodom on its judgment-day;
(Amen.)
Moses from the land of bondage and despair;
(Amen.)
Daniel from the hungry lions in their lair;
(Amen.)
And the Children Three amid the furnace-flame;
(Amen.)
Chaste Susanna from the slander and the shame;
(Amen.)
David from Golia and the wrath of Saul;
(Amen.)
And the two Apostles from their prison-thrall;
(Amen.)
Thecla from her torments;
(Amen:)
—so to show Thy power,
Rescue this Thy servant in his evil hour.

GERONTIUS

Novissima hora est; and I fain would sleep.
The pain has wearied me...Into Thy hands,
O Lord, into Thy hands...

THE PRIEST

Proficiscere, anima Christiana, de hoc mundo!
Go forth upon thy journey, Christian soul!
Go from this world! Go, in the Name of God
The Omnipotent Father, who created thee!
Go, in the Name of Jesus Christ, our Lord,
Son of the living God, who bled for thee!
Go, in the Name of the Holy Spirit, who
Hath been pour'd out on thee! Go, in the name
Of Angels and Archangels; in the name
Of Thrones and Dominations; in the name
Of Princedoms and of Powers; and in the name
Of Cherubim and Seraphim, go forth!
Go, in the name of Patriarchs and Prophets;
And of Apostles and Evangelists,
Of Martyrs and Confessors; in the name
Of holy Monks and Hermits; in the name
Of holy Virgins; and all Saints of God,
Both men and women, go! Go on thy course;
And may thy place to-day be found in peace,
And may thy dwelling be the Holy Mount
Of Sion:—through the Same, through Christ, our Lord.

§2

SOUL OF GERONTIUS

I WENT to sleep; and now I am refresh'd,
A strange refreshment: for I feel in me
An inexpressive lightness, and a sense
Of freedom, as I were at length myself,
And ne'er had been before. How still it is!
I hear no more the busy beat of time,
No, nor my fluttering breath, nor struggling pulse;
Nor does one moment differ from the next.
I had a dream; yes:— some one softly said
"He's gone;" and then a sigh went round the room.
And then I surely heard a priestly voice
Cry "Subvenite;" and they knelt in prayer.
I seem to hear him still; but thin and low,

And fainter and more faint the accents come,
As at an ever-widening interval.
Ah! whence is this? What is this severance?
This silence pours a solitariness
Into the very essence of my soul;
And the deep rest, so soothing and so sweet,
Hath something too of sternness and of pain.
For it drives back my thoughts upon their spring
By a strange introversion, and perforce
I now begin to feed upon myself,
Because I have nought else to feed upon.

Am I alive or dead? I am not dead,
But in the body still; for I possess
A sort of confidence, which clings to me,
That each particular organ holds its place
As heretofore, combining with the rest
Into one symmetry, that wraps me round,
And makes me man; and surely I could move,
Did I but will it, every part of me.
And yet I cannot to my sense bring home
By very trial, that I have the power.
'Tis strange; I cannot stir a hand or foot,
I cannot make my fingers or my lips
By mutual pressure witness each to each,
Nor by the eyelid's instantaneous stroke
Assure myself I have a body still.
Nor do I know my very attitude,
Nor if I stand, or lie, or sit, or kneel.

So much I know, not knowing how I know,
That the vast universe, where I have dwelt,
Is quitting me, or I am quitting it.
Or I or it is rushing on the wings
Of light or lightning on an inward course,
And we e'en now are million miles apart.
Yet…is this peremptory severance
Wrought out in lengthening measurements of space,
Which grow and multiply by speed and time?

Or am I traversing infinity
By endlesss subdivision, hurrying back
From finite towards infinitesimal,
Thus dying out of the expanded world?

Another marvel: someone has me fast
Within his ample palm; 'tis not a grasp
Such as they use on earth, but all around
Over the surface of my subtle being,
As though I were a sphere, and capable
To be accosted thus, a uniform
And gentle pressure tells me I am not
Self-moving, but borne forward on my way.
And hark! I hear a singing; yet in sooth
I cannot of that music rightly say
Whether I hear, or touch, or taste the tones.
Oh, what a heart-subduing melody!

ANGEL

My work is done,
My task is o'er,
And so I come,
Taking it home,
For the crown is won,
Alleluia,
For evermore.

My Father gave
In charge to me
This child of earth
E'en from its birth,
To serve and save,
Alleluia,
And saved is he.

This child of clay
To me was given,
To rear and train
By sorrow and pain
In the narrow way,
Alleluia.
From earth to heaven.

SOUL

It is a member of that family
Of wondrous beings, who, ere the worlds were made,
Millions of ages back, have stood around
The throne of God:—he never has known sin;
But through those cycles all but infinite,
Has had a strong and pure celestial life,
And bore to gaze on the unveil'd face of God,
And drank from the everlasting Fount of truth,
And served Him with a keen ecstatic love.
Hark! he begins again.

ANGEL

O Lord, how wonderful in depth and height,
But most in man, how wonderful Thou art!
With what a love, what soft persuasive might
Victorious o'er the stubborn fleshly heart,
Thy tale complete of saints Thou dost provide,
To fill the throne which Angels lost through pride!

He lay a grovelling babe upon the ground,
Polluted in the blood of his first sire,
With his whole essence shatter'd and unsound,
And coil'd around his heart a demon dire,
Which was not of his nature, but had skill
To bind and form his op'ning mind to ill.

Then was I sent from heaven to set right
The balance in his soul of truth and sin,
And I have waged a long relentless fight,
Resolved that death-environ'd spirit to win,
Which from its fallen state, when all was lost,
Had been repurchased at so dread a cost.

Oh, what a shifting parti-colour'd scene
Of hope and fear, of triumph and dismay,
Of recklessness and penitence, has been
The history of that dreary, life-long fray!
And oh, the grace to nerve him and to lead,
How patient, prompt, and lavish at his need!

O man, strange composite of heaven and earth!
Majesty dwarf'd to baseness! fragrant flower
Running to poisonous seed! and seeming worth
Cloking corruption! weakness mastering power!
Who never art so near to crime and shame,
As when thou hast achieved some deed of name;—

How should ethereal natures comprehend
A thing made up of spirit and of clay,
Were we not task'd to nurse it and to tend,
Link'd one to one throughout its mortal day?
More than the Seraph in his height of place,
The Angel-guardian knows and loves the ransom'd race..

SOUL

Now know I surely that I am at length
Out of the body; had I part with earth,
I never could have drunk those accents in,
And not have worshipp'd as a god the voice
That was so musical; but now I am
So whole of heart, so calm, so self-possess'd,
With such a full content, and with a sense
So apprehensive and discriminant,
As no temptation can intoxicate.
Nor have I even terror at the thought
That I am clasp'd by such a saintliness.

ANGEL

All praise to Him, at whose sublime decree
  The last are first, the first become the last;
By whom the suppliant prisoner is set free,
  By whom proud first-borns from their thrones are cast;
Who raises Mary to be Queen of heaven,
While Lucifer is left, condemn'd and unforgiven.

§3

SOUL

I WILL address him. Mighty one, my Lord,
My Guardian Spirit, all hail!

ANGEL

All hail, my child!
My child and brother, hail! what wouldest thou?

SOUL

I would have nothing but to speak with thee
For speaking's sake. I wish to hold with thee
Conscious communion; though I fain would know
A maze of things, were it but meet to ask,
And not a curiousness.

ANGEL

You cannot now
Cherish a wish which ought not to be wish'd.

SOUL

Then I will speak. I ever had believed
That on the moment when the struggling soul
Quitted its mortal case, forthwith it fell
Under the awful Presence of its God,
There to be judged and sent to its own place.
What lets me now from going to my Lord?

ANGEL

Thou art not let; but with extremest speed
Art hurrying to the Just and Holy Judge:
For scarcely art thou disembodied yet.
Divide a moment, as men measure time,
Into its million-million-millionth part,
Yet even less than that the interval
Since thou didst leave the body; and the priest
Cried "Subvenite," and they fell to prayer;
Nay, scarcely yet have they begun to pray.

For spirits and men by different standards mete
The less and greater in the flow of time.
By sun and moon, primeval ordinances—
By stars which rise and set harmoniously—
By the recurring seasons, and the swing,
This way and that, of the suspended rod
Precise and punctual, men divide the hours,
Equal, continuous, for their common use.
Not so with us in the immaterial world;
But intervals in their succession
Are measured by the living thought alone
And grow or wane with its intensity.
And time is not a common property;
But what is long is short, and swift is slow,
And near is distant, as received and grasp'd
By this mind and by that, and every one

Is standard of his own chronology.
And memory lacks its natural resting-points
Of years, and centuries, and periods.
It is thy very energy of thought
Which keeps thee from thy God.

SOUL

Dear Angel, say,
Why have I now no fear at meeting Him?
Along my earthly life, the thought of death
And judgment was to me most terrible.
I had it aye before me, and I saw
The Judge severe e'en in the Crucifix.
Now that the hour is come, my fear is fled;
And at this balance of my destiny,
Now close upon me, I can forward look
With a serenest joy.

ANGEL

It is because
Then thou didst fear, that now thou dost not fear,
Thou hast forestall'd the agony, and so
For thee the bitterness of death is past.
Also, because already in thy soul
The judgment is begun. That day of doom,
One and the same for the collected world—
That solemn consummation for all flesh,
Is, in the case of each, anticipate
Upon his death; and, as the last great day
In the particular judgment is rehearsed,
So now, too, ere thou comest to the Throne,
A presage falls upon thee, as a ray
Straight from the Judge, expressive of thy lot.
That calm and joy uprising in thy soul
Is first-fruit to thee of thy recompense,
And heaven begun.

§4

SOUL

But hark! upon my sense
Comes a fierce hubbub, which would make me fear,
Could I be frighted.

ANGEL

We are now arrived
Close on the judgment-court; that sullen howl
Is from the demons who assemble there.
It is the middle region, where of old
Satan appeared among the sons of God,
To cast his jibes and scoffs at holy Job.
So now his legions throng the vestibule,
Hungry and wild, to claim their property,
And gather souls for hell. Hist to their cry.

SOUL

How sour and how uncouth a dissonance!

DEMONS

Low-born clods
Of brute earth,
They aspire
To become gods,
By a new birth,
And an extra grace,
And a score of merits,
As if aught
Could stand in place
Of the high thought,
And the glance of fire
Of the great spirits,
The powers blest,
The lords by right,
The primal owners,
Of the proud dwelling

And realm of light,—
Dispossess'd,
Aside thrust,
Chuck'd down
By the sheer might
Of a despot's will,
Of a tyrant's frown,
Who after expelling
Their hosts, gave,
Triumphant still,
And still unjust,
Each forfeit crown
To psalm-droners,
And canting groaners,
To every slave,
And pious cheat,
And crawling knave,
Who lick'd the dust
Under his feet.

ANGEL

It is the restless panting of their being;
Like beasts of prey, who, caged within their bars,
In a deep hideous purring have their life,
And an incessant pacing to and fro.

DEMONS

The mind bold
And independent,
The purpose free,
So we are told,
Must not think
To have the ascendant.
What's a saint?
One whose breath
Doth the air taint
Before his death;
A bundle of bones,

Which fools adore,
Ha! ha!
When life is o'er;
Which rattle and stink,
E'en in the flesh.
We cry his pardon!
No flesh hath he;
Ha! ha!
For it hath died,
'Tis crucified
Day by day,
Afresh, afresh,
Ha! ha!
That holy clay,
Ha! ha!
This gains guerdon,
So priestlings prate,
Ha! ha!
Before the Judge,
And pleads and atones
For spite and grudge,
And bigot mood,
And envy and hate,
And greed of blood.

SOUL

How impotent they are! and yet on earth
They have repute for wondrous power and skill;
And books describe, how that the very face
Of the Evil One, if seen, would have a force
Even to freeze the blood, and choke the life
Of him who saw it.

ANGEL

In thy trial-state
Thou hadst a traitor nestling close at home,
Connatural, who with the powers of hell
Was leagued, and of thy senses kept the keys,
And to that deadliest foe unlock'd thy heart.

And therefore is it, in respect of man,
Those fallen ones show so majestical.
But, when some child of grace, Angel or Saint,
Pure and upright in his integrity
Of nature, meets the demons on their raid,
They scud away as cowards from the fight.
Nay, oft hath holy hermit in his cell,
Not yet disburden'd of mortality,
Mock'd at their threats and warlike overtures;
Or, dying, when they swarm'd, like flies, around,
Defied them, and departed to his Judge.

DEMONS

Virtue and vice,
A knave's pretence,
'Tis all the same;
Ha! Ha!
Dread of hell-fire,
Of the venomous flame,
A coward's plea.
Give him his price,
Saint though he be,

Ha! Ha!
From shrewd good sense
He'll slave for hire;
Ha! ha!
And does but aspire
To the heaven above
With sordid aim,
And not from love.
Ha! ha!

SOUL

I see not those false spirits; shall I see
My dearest Master, when I reach His throne?
Or hear, at least, His awful judgment-word
With personal intonation, as I now
Hear thee, not see thee, Angel? Hitherto
All has been darkness since I left the earth;
Shall I remain thus sight-bereft all through
My penance-time? If so, how comes it then
That I have hearing still, and taste, and touch,
Yet not a glimmer of that princely sense
Which binds ideas in one, and makes them live?

ANGEL

Nor touch, nor taste, nor hearing hast thou now;
Thou livest in a world of signs and types,
The presentations of most holy truths,
Living and strong, which now encompass thee.
A disembodied soul, thou hast by right
No converse with aught else beside thyself;
But, lest so stern a solitude should load
And break thy being, in mercy are vouchsafed
Some lower measures of perception,
Which seem to thee, as though through channels brought,
Through ear, or nerves, or palate, which are gone.
And thou art wrapp'd and swathed around in dreams,
Dreams that are true, yet enigmatical;
For the belongings of thy present state,
Save through such symbols, come not home to thee.

And thus thou tell'st of space, and time, and size,
Of fragrant, solid, bitter, musical,
Of fire, and of refreshment after fire;
As (let me use similitude of earth,
To aid thee in the knowledge thou dost ask)—
As ice which blisters may be said to burn.
Nor hast thou now extension, with its parts
Correlative,—long habit cozens thee,—
Nor power to move thyself, nor limbs to move
Hast thou not heard of those, who after loss
Of hand or foot, as though they had it still?
So is it now with thee, who hast not lost
Thy hand or foot, but all which made up man.
So will it be, until the joyous day
Of resurrection, when thou wilt regain
All thou hast lost, new-made and glorified.
How, even now, the consummated Saints
See God in heaven, I may not explicate;
Meanwhile, let it suffice thee to possess
Such means of converse as are granted thee,
Though, till that Beatific Vision, thou art blind;
For e'en thy purgatory, which comes like fire,
Is fire without its light.

SOUL

His will be done!
I am not worthy e'er to see again
The face of day; far less His countenance,
Who is the very sun. Natheless in life,
When I look'd forward to my purgatory,
It ever was my solace to believe,
That, ere I plunged amid the avenging flame,
I had one sight of Him to strengthen me.

ANGEL

Nor rash nor vain is that presentiment;
Yes,—for one moment thou shalt see thy Lord.
Thus will it be: what time thou art arraign'd
Before the dread tribunal, and thy lot

Is cast for ever, should it be to sit
On His right hand among His pure elect,
Then sight, or that which to the soul is sight,
As by a lightning-flash, will come to thee,
And thou shalt see, amid the dark profound,
Whom thy soul loveth, and would fain approach,—
One moment; but thou knowest not, my child,
What thou dost ask: that sight of the Most Fair
Will gladden thee, but it will pierce thee too.

SOUL

Thou speakest darkly, Angel; and an awe
Falls on me, and a fear lest I be rash.

ANGEL

There was a mortal, who is now above
In the mid glory: he, when near to die,
Was given communion with the Crucified,—
Such, that the Master's very wounds were stamp'd
Upon his flesh; and, from the agony
Which thrill'd through body and soul in that embrace,
Learn that the flame of the Everlasting Love
Doth burn ere it transform...

§5

HARK to those sounds!
...They come of tender beings angelical,
Least and most childlike of the sons of God.

FIRST CHOIR OF ANGELICALS

Praise to the Holiest in the height,
And in the depth be praise:
In all His words most wonderful;
Most sure in all His ways!

To us His elder race He gave
  To battle and to win,
Without the chastisement of pain,
  Without the soil of sin.

The younger son He will'd to be
  A marvel in his birth:
Spirit and flesh his parents were;
  His home was heaven and earth.

The Eternal bless'd His child, and arm'd,
  And sent him hence afar,
To serve as champion in the field
  Of elemental war.

To be His Viceroy in the world
  Of matter, and of sense;
Upon the frontier, towards the foe,
  A resolute defence.

ANGEL

We now have pass'd the gate, and are within
The House of Judgment; and whereas on earth
Temples and palaces are form'd of parts
Costly and rare, but all material,
So in the world of spirits nought is found,
To mould withal, and form into a whole,
But what is immaterial; and thus
The smallest portions of this edifice,
Cornice, or frieze, or balustrade, or stair,
The very pavement is made up of life—
Of holy, blessed, and immortal beings,
Who hymn their Maker's praise continually.

SECOND CHOIR OF ANGELICALS

Praise to the Holiest in the height,
  And in the depth be praise:
In all His words most wonderful;
  Most sure in all His ways!

Woe to thee, man! for he was found
  A recreant in the fight;
And lost his heritage of heaven,
  And fellowship with light.

Above him now the angry sky,
  Around the tempest's din;
Who once had Angels for his friends,
Had but the brutes for kin.

O man! a savage kindred they;
  To flee that monster brood
He scaled the seaside cave, and clomb
  The giants of the wood.

With now a fear, and now a hope,
  With aids which chance supplied,
From youth to eld, from sire to son,
  He lived, and toil'd, and died.

He dreed his penance age by age;
  And step by step began
Slowly to doff his savage garb,
  And be again a man.

And quicken'd by the Almighty's breath
  And chasten'd by His rod,
And taught by angel-visitings,
  At length he sought his God;

And learn'd to call upon His Name,
  And in His faith create
A household and a father-land,
  A city and a state.

Glory to Him who from the mire,
  In patient length of days,
Elaborated into life
  A people to His praise!

SOUL

The sound is like the rushing of the wind—
The summer wind—among the lofty pines;
Swelling and dying, echoing round about,
Now here, now distant, wild and beautiful;
While, scatter'd from the branches it has stirr'd,
Descend ecstatic odours.

THIRD CHOIR OF ANGELICALS

Praise to the Holiest in the height,
  And in the depth be praise:
In all His words most wonderful;
  Most sure in all His ways!

The Angels, as beseemingly
  To spirit-kind was given,
At once were tried and perfected,
  And took their seats in heaven.

For them no twilight or eclipse;
  No growth and no decay:
'Twas hopeless, all-ingulfing night,
  Or beatific day.

But to the younger race there rose
  A hope upon its fall;
And slowly, surely, gracefully,
  The morning dawn'd on all.

And ages, opening out, divide
  The precious and the base,
And from the hard and sullen mass
  Mature the heirs of grace.

O man! albeit the quickening ray
  Lit from his second birth,
Makes him at length what once he was,
  And heaven grows out of earth;

Yet still between that earth and heaven—
  His journey and his goal—
A double agony awaits
  His body and his soul.

A double debt he has to pay—
  The forfeit of his sins:
The chill of death is past, and now
  The penance-fire begins.

Glory to Him; who evermore
  By truth and justice reigns;
Who tears the soul from out its case,
  And burns away its stains!

ANGEL

They sing of thy approaching agony,
Which thou so eagerly didst question of:
It is the face of the Incarnate God
Shall smite thee with that keen and subtle pain;
And yet the memory which it leaves will be
A sovereign febrifuge to heal the wound;
And yet withal it will the wound provoke,
And aggravate and widen it the more.

SOUL

Thou speakest mysteries; still methinks I know
To disengage the tangle of thy words:
Yet rather would I hear thy angel voice,
Than for myself be thy interpreter.

ANGEL

When then—if such thy lot—thou seest thy Judge,
The sight of Him will kindle in thy heart
All tender, gracious, reverential thoughts.
Thou wilt be sick with love, and yearn for Him,
And feel as though thou couldst but pity Him,
That one so sweet should e'er have placed Himself
At disadvantage such, as to be used
So vilely by a being so vile as thee.
There is a pleading in His pensive eyes
Will pierce thee to the quick, and trouble thee.
And thou wilt hate and loathe thyself; for, though
Now sinless, thou wilt feel that thou hast sinn'd,
As never thou didst feel; and wilt desire
To slink away, and hide thee from His sight:
And yet wilt have a longing aye to dwell
Within the beauty of His countenance.
And these two pains, so counter and so keen,—
The longing for Him, when thou seest Him not;
The shame of self at thought of seeing Him,—
Will be thy veriest, sharpest purgatory.

SOUL

My soul is in my hand: I have no fear,—
In His dear might prepared for weal or woe.
But hark! a grand, mysterious harmony:
It floods me like the deep and solemn sound
Of many waters.

ANGEL

We have gain'd the stairs
Which rise towards the Presence-chamber; there
A band of mighty Angels keep the way
On either side, and hymn the Incarnate God.

ANGELS OF THE SACRED STAIR

Father, whose goodness none can know, but they
Who see Thee face to face,
By man hath come the infinite display
Of Thy victorious grace;
But fallen man—the creature of a day—
Skills not that love to trace.
It needs, to tell the triumph Thou hast wrought,
An Angel's deathless fire, an Angel's reach of thought.

It needs that very Angel, who with awe,
Amid the garden shade,
The great Creator in His sickness saw,
Soothed by a creature's aid,
And agonized, as victim of the Law
Which He Himself had made;
For who can praise Him in his depth and height,
But he who saw Him reel amid that solitary fight?

SOUL

Hark! for the lintels of the presence-gate
Are vibrating and echoing back the strain.

FOURTH CHOIR OF ANGELICALS

Praise to the Holiest in the height,
And in the depth be praise;
In all His words most wonderful;
Most sure in all His ways!

The foe blasphemed the Holy Lord,
As if He reckon'd ill,
In that He placed His puppet man
The frontier place to fill.

For, even in his best estate,
  With amplest gifts endued,
A sorry sentinel was he,
  A being of flesh and blood.

As though a thing, who for his help
  Must needs possess a wife,
Could cope with those proud rebel hosts
  Who had angelic life.

And when, by blandishment of Eve,
  That earth-born Adam fell,
He shriek'd in triumph, and he cried,
  "A sorry sentinel;

"The Maker by His word is bound,
  Escape or cure is none;
He must abandon to his doom,
  And slay His darling son."

ANGEL

And now the threshold, as we traverse it,
Utters aloud its glad responsive chant.

FIFTH CHOIR OF ANGELICALS

Praise to the Holiest in the height,
  And in the depth be praise:
In all His words most wonderful;
  Most sure in all His ways!

O loving wisdom of our God!
  When all was sin and shame,
A second Adam to the fight
  And to the rescue came.

O wisest love! that flesh and blood
  Which did in Adam fail,
Should strive afresh against their foe,
  Should strive and should prevail;

And that a higher gift than grace
  Should flesh and blood refine,
God's Presence and His very Self,
  And Essence all-divine.

O generous love! that He who smote
  In man for man the foe,
The double agony in man
  For man should undergo;

And in the garden secretly,
  And on the cross on high,
Should teach His brethren and inspire
  To suffer and to die.

§6

ANGEL

THY judgment now is near, for we are come
Into the veilèd presence of our God.

SOUL

I hear the voices that I left on earth.

ANGEL

It is the voice of friends around thy bed,
Who say the "Subvenite" with the priest.
Hither the echoes come; before the Throne
Stands the great Angel of the Agony,
The same who strengthen'd Him, what time He knelt
Lone in that garden shade, bedew'd with blood.
That Angel best can plead with Him for all
Tormented souls, the dying and the dead.

ANGEL OF THE AGONY

Jesu! by that shuddering dread which fell on Thee;
Jesu! by that cold dismay which sicken'd Thee;
Jesu! by that pang of heart which thrill'd in Thee;
Jesu! by that mount of sins which crippled Thee;
Jesu! by that sense of guilt which stifled Thee;
Jesu! by that innocence which girdled Thee;
Jesu! by that sanctity which reign'd in Thee;
Jesu! by that Godhead which was one with Thee;
Jesu! spare these souls which are so dear to Thee,
Who in prison, calm and patient, wait for Thee;
Hasten, Lord, their hour, and bid them come to Thee,
To that glorious Home, where they shall ever gaze on Thee.

SOUL

I go before my Judge. Ah!...

ANGEL

...Praise to His Name!
The eager spirit has darted from my hold,
And, with intemperate energy of love,
Flies to the dear feet of Emmanuel;
But, ere it reach them, the keen sanctity,
Which with its effluence, like a glory, clothes
And circles round the Crucified, has seized,
And scorch'd, and shrivell'd it; and now it lies
Passive and still before the awful Throne.
O happy, suffering soul! for it is safe,
Consumed, yet quicken'd, by the glance of God.

SOUL

Take me away, and in the lowest deep
        There let me be,
And there in hope the lone night-watches keep,
        Told out for me.
There, motionless and happy in my pain,
        Lone, not forlorn,—
There will I sing my sad perpetual strain,
        Until the morn.
There will I sing, and soothe my stricken breast,
        Which ne'er can cease
To throb, and pine, and languish, till possest
        Of its Sole Peace.
There will I sing my absent Lord and Love:—
        Take me away,
That sooner I may rise, and go above,
And see Him in the truth of everlasting day.

§7

ANGEL

Now let the golden prison ope its gates,
Making sweet music, as each fold revolves
Upon its ready hinge. And ye, great powers,
Angels of Purgatory, receive from me
My charge, a precious soul, until the day,
When, from all bond and forfeiture released,
I shall reclaim it for the courts of light.

SOULS IN PURGATORY

1. Lord, Thou hast been our refuge: in every generation;

2. Before the hills were born, and the world was: from age to age Thou art God.

3. Bring us not, Lord, very low: for Thou hast said, Come back again, ye sons of Adam.

4. A thousand years before Thine eyes are but as yesterday: and as a watch of the night which is come and gone.

5. The grass springs up in the morning: at evening-tide it shrivels up and dies.

6. So we fail in Thine anger: and in Thy wrath are we troubled.

7. Thou hast set our sins in Thy sight: and our round of days in the light of Thy countenance.

8. Come back, O Lord! how long: and be entreated for Thy servants.

9. In Thy morning we shall be filled with Thy mercy: we shall rejoice and be in pleasure all our days.

10. We shall be glad according to the days of our humiliation: and the years in which we have seen evil.

11. Look, O Lord, upon Thy servants and on Thy work: and direct their children.

12. And let the beauty of the Lord our God be upon us: and the work of our hands, establish Thou it.

Glory be to the Father, and to the Son: and to the Holy Ghost. As it was in the beginning, is now, and ever shall be: world without end. Amen.

ANGEL

Softly and gently, dearly-ransom'd soul,
  In my most loving arms I now enfold thee,
And, o'er the penal waters, as they roll,
  I poise thee, and I lower thee, and hold thee.

And carefully I dip thee in the lake,
  And thou, without a sob or a resistance,
Dost through the flood thy rapid passage take,
  Sinking deep, deeper, into the dim distance.

Angels, to whom the willing task is given,
  Shall tend, and nurse, and lull thee, as thou liest;
And Masses on the earth, and prayers in heaven,
  Shall aid thee at the Throne of the Most Highest.

Farewell, but not for ever! brother dear,
  Be brave and patient on thy bed of sorrow;
Swiftly shall pass thy night of trial here,
  And I will come and wake thee on the morrow.

The Oratory. *January, 1865*

INDEX OF FIRST LINES